## Date Due

| 9/25/53 | | | |
|---|---|---|---|
| 1-24-56 | | | |
| | | | |
| | | | |
| | | | |
| | | | |
| | | | |
| | | | |
| | | | |
| | | | |
| | | | |
| | | | |
| | | | |
| | | | |
| | | | |
| | | | |
| | | | |

# THE HORSE AND THE SWORD

By HAROLD PEAKE and
HERBERT JOHN FLEURE

NEW HAVEN · YALE UNIVERSITY PRESS
LONDON · HUMPHREY MILFORD
OXFORD UNIVERSITY PRESS
1933

# PREFACE

It may not be out of place to point out here that the purpose of these volumes, 'The Corridors of Time', is less to provide a popular account of prehistoric times to those wholly new to the subject, than to help the serious student, who is not a specialist, to obtain a general view of the sequence of events in these far off times, and we have ventured to hope that even the specialist might by their help be enabled to see his own particular field of work in more correct perspective.

The old division of prehistoric times into the Stone, Bronze, and Iron Ages, though it has been of inestimable value during the last century in bringing a measure of order out of chaos, is now revealing signs of failure to meet the needs of to-day. This volume endeavours to show that the transition from the Middle to the Late Bronze Age in Europe was a period of crisis, of far greater importance than the transition from the use of bronze to that of iron. Henceforth men on horseback, armed with swords, were to organize and govern the peasant communities of Europe and Asia; under their rule, civilization in Central Europe was to rise to a higher level, while the lands around the Western Baltic were to develop a fine display of craftsmanship.

The brilliant promise of these early civilizations in our continent was cut off by the advent of a cold and wet period; and the climatic change led, at the same time, to enlargement of the opportunities of the Mediterranean lands, better secured under these conditions from the effects of prolonged drought.

It was the arrival on the scene of the horse and the sword, it would appear, rather than the introduction of weapons of iron, that caused these great developments in the social structure of Europe: the severe crisis that followed some centuries later was in a great measure due to climatic change.

At this period legendary history begins to supplement the

archaeological record, and we attach great importance to these stories handed down by folk memory, since they appear to give a broad version of truth, though often accompanied by fanciful details.

The next and last volume of this chronological series will continue the story to the time that witnessed the rise of law-givers, prophets, and philosophers; the teachings of these sages caused abstract ideas to begin to wing their own way, and it becomes impossible to treat later history by the methods we have hitherto employed. The chronological series will be followed by a final volume, giving a general survey of the whole subject with emphasis on the more important milestones marking the way of human progress.

Many thanks are due to the authors, editors, and publishers of the following works and journals for permission to reproduce figures: *The Aegean Civilization*, by G. Glotz (Kegan Paul, Trench, Trübner & Co., Ltd.) for figs. 5 and 18; *Catalogue of the Greek and Etruscan Vases in the British Museum*, vol. i, pt. i, for fig. 6; *A Guide to the Antiquities of the Bronze Age* (British Museum), for fig. 54; *The British Museum Quarterly*, vol. ii, No. 1, for fig. 25a; *Catalogue of Bronzes in the Eumorphopoulos Collection*, vol. i (Ernest Benn, Ltd.), for fig. 62; *Fibules grecques et orientales*, by Chr. Blinkenberg (Danish Academy, Copenhagen), and *Who Were the Greeks?*, by J. L. Myres (University of California Press), for figs. 7 and 33; *Troja und Ilion*, 2 vols., by W. Dörpfeld (German Archaeological Institute, Athens), for figs. 8, 14, and 16; *Tiryns*, by G. Rodenwaldt (German Archaeological Institute, Athens), for fig. 17; *A History of Egypt*, 2nd edition, by J. H. Breasted (Scribner's Sons, New York; Hodder & Stoughton, Ltd., London), for figs. 10 and 21; *A History of Babylon*, by L. W. King (Chatto & Windus), for fig. 11; *Tools and Weapons*, by Professor Sir Flinders Petrie (Bernard Quaritch, Ltd.), for fig. 12; *Annual of the British School at Athens*, No. xxvii, for fig. 23; *Ilios*, by H. Schliemann (John Murray), for fig. 24; *Reallexikon der Vorgeschichte*, vols. iii, iv, viii, ix, x, xi, xii, and xiv (Walter de Gruyter & Co., Berlin), for figs. 25b and c, 28, 37c,

42, 44, 46, 47, 48a, and 53; *The Danube in Prehistory*, by V. Gordon Childe (Clarendon Press), for figs. 26, 27 and 34; *Die vorrömischen Schwerter*, by Julius Naue (Piloty & Loehle, Munich), for figs. 29, 31, 32, 38–40, and 43; *The Bronze Age and the Celtic World*, by Harold Peake (Ernest Benn Ltd.), for fig. 30; *Ancient Bronze Implements*, by J. Evans (Longmans, Green & Co., Ltd.), for figs. 35 and 58; *Antiquity*, March 1928 and June 1930, for figs. 36 and 59; *The Stone and Bronze Ages in Italy*, by T. E. Peet (Clarendon Press), for fig. 37b; *Die Kultur der Bronzezeit in Süddeutschland*, by G. Kraft (Verlag Dr. Benno Filser, Augsburg), for fig. 41; *Les temps préhistoriques en Suède*, by O. Montelius (Librairie E. Leroux, Paris), for fig. 45; *Oldtidens Kunst, Bronzealderen*, by S. Müller (H. H. Thieles, Copenhagen), for figs. 48b and 49–52; *Bronze Age Pottery*, vol. ii, by J. Abercromby (Clarendon Press), for figs. 55 and 56; *Man*, vol. xxxi (Royal Anthropological Institute of Great Britain & Ireland), for fig. 57 and *Monumenti Antichi* (Reale Accademia Nazionale dei Lincei, Rome) for fig. 37a.

# CONTENTS

1. A Period of Change . . . . . . 1

2. The Near East in the Fourteenth Century B.C. . 9

3. The Near East in the Thirteenth Century B.C. . 24

4. The Tale of Troy . . . . . . 40

5. The Near East in the Twelfth Century B.C. . . 56

6. The Near East in the Eleventh Century B.C. . . 69

7. East-Central Europe . . . . . . 80

8. Italy in the Late Bronze Age . . . . 95

9. West-Central and North-West Europe . . . 103

10. Atlantic Europe . . . . . . . 122

11. The Monsoon Lands of Asia . . . . 135

12. General Summary . . . . . . 142

INDEX . . . . . . . . . 149

# LIST OF ILLUSTRATIONS

1. Map of Greece, showing the distribution of dialects in the
thirteenth century . . . . . . . 4
2. Map of northern Greece . . . . . . . 7
3. The Temple and Tomb of Minos. Photograph by courtesy of
Sir Arthur Evans . . . . . . . . 10
4. Map of Greece about 1400 B.C. . . . . . . 12
5. Bull-leaping fresco at Knossos . . . . . . 14
6. Vases of the Third Late Minoan period . . . . 16
7. Catch-pin from Crete. From Myres, after Blinkenberg . . 17
8. Plan of Hissarlik VI. . . . . . . . 19
9. Chronological chart of the kings in the Near East . . 21
10. Scene from the reliefs of the Battle of Kadesh . . . 28
11. Figure, probably of a Hittite king, from the royal gate at
Khattussas . . . . . . . . . 31
12. Bronze sword, bearing the cartouche of Seti II . . . 35
13. Figures of frenzied women dancing. Photograph, Lam-
brinides . . . . . . . . . 38
14. The water tower at Troy . . . . . . . 43
15. Map of the Aegean region at the time of the Trojan War . 45
16. Plan of a megaron . . . . . . . . 50
17. A war chariot at Mycenae . . . . . . 52
18. Warlike equipment of the Achaeans . . . . . 54
19. Philistines defeated by Egyptians and Shardana. After
Champollion. . . . . . . . . 57
20. Map of the Near East . . . . . . . 62
21. Ramses IX decorating Amenhotep, High Priest of Amon . 65
22. Divine emblems on a charter of Nebuchadrezzar I. British
Museum . . . . . . . . . 67
23. Pottery from Vardaroftsa . . . . . . 71
24. Lausitz pottery from Hissarlik VII . . . . . 72
25. Various types of geometric pottery . . . . . 77
26. Bronze battle-axes from Hungary . . . . . 81
27. The Urn-field culture and its pottery. *a, b* from Lovasberény,
*c* from Temes-Kubin . . . . . . . 83
28. Examples of Pannonian ware . . . . . . 84
29. Sword with full metal hilt, derived from dagger . . . 86
30. Sword with spiral ornament on blade . . . . . 87
31. Tongue-grip swords from Hungary . . . . . 88
32. Sword with full metal hilt, in cast metal . . . . 89

33. A bent pin and fibulae. From Myres, after Blinkenberg . 90
34. Fibulae . . . . . . . . . . 91
35. A winged axe and a socketed axe with wings marked . . 91
36. A view of the origin of the socketed axe . . . . 93
37. Bronze razors from Sicily. *a* after Orsi, *Mon. Ant.* . . 99
38. Bronze swords from Italy . . . . . . . 101
39. Bronze swords from Sulmona, Trasimene, and Apulia . . 102
40. Swords with octagonal hilts . . . . . . 105
41. South German Tumulus pottery . . . . . 106
42. Bronze Age pins from Jura and Aveyron, France . . 108
43. Mörigen and Auvernier types of swords . . . . 110
44. Objects from the Swiss pile-dwellings . . . . . 111
45. Ornamental flanged axe . . . . . . . 113
46. Danish dagger and short swords . . . . . 114
47. Axes and swords from the Baltic area . . . . 115
48. Camp-stool, and two-piece safety-pin . . . . 116
49. *Tutulus* . . . . . . . . . . 117
50. Battle-axe and swords . . . . . . . 118
51. Bronze horse and disk . . . . . . . 119
52. Late Bronze Age objects from Denmark . . . . 120
53. Rock drawings from Sweden . . . . . . 121
54. Food-vessels . . . . . . . . . 123
55. British cinerary urns . . . . . . . 124
56. Deverel-Rimbury urns . . . . . . . 125
57. Map showing the distribution of winged axes in France and England . . . . . . . . . 127
58. Socketed axes from *a* Alfriston and *b, c* Ireland . . . 129
59. Distribution of swords, Beachy Head type . . . . 131
60. Map of the Punjab . . . . . . . . 136
61. Impression of seal from Eshnunna. Photograph by courtesy of Dr. H. Frankfort . . . . . . . 137
62. A bronze dating from the Chou Dynasty . . . . 141

# A Period of Change

OUR last volume, *Merchant Venturers in Bronze*, dealt with the period during which the use of bronze, an alloy of copper and tin, was spreading from Hissarlik all over Europe and the Near East, giving rise to fresh developments in the civilization of the West, while in Egypt and Asia Minor empires flourished and expanded, and a great mercantile state grew up in Crete and the neighbouring isles. That volume carried our history of civilization down to 1400 B.C., when the fall of Knossos brought Cretan power to an end, and to 1350 B.C. in Egypt, when its 18th Dynasty terminated soon after the death of Tut-enkh-amon.

Here we shall continue this history for about 400 years, during which we witness the death-throes of the Bronze Age civilization and the birth of those forces that were to mould the life of the Classical Age.

This period of 400 years falls into two equal and sharply defined phases, but before discussing these we must first of all determine the date of an important episode, which serves as a turning-point, the siege and sack of Troy.

Two very important works, dealing with Greek lands during these dark ages, have recently appeared. One, by a brilliant young author hitherto unknown to fame, sets forth a new view as to the date of this famous episode. Mr. Burn argues that the chronologies compiled by Eratosthenes and later Greek historians are not to be trusted, partly because these are based upon pedigrees, not always reliable in themselves, and partly because in them too many years are reckoned to a generation. Therefore Mr. Burn rejects the date of the Trojan War as given by Eratosthenes, and believes that this campaign took place somewhere about 1100 B.C.

On the other hand Professor Myres, who has recently

3093.8                        B

brought out a large volume on this period, has a great respect for the accuracy of these pedigrees, at least of those that appear in early works. He believes, with Eratosthenes, that the Trojan War took place between 1194 and 1184 B.C. Our readers know that we have paid the greatest respect to tradition; we therefore agree with Myres rather than with Burn, though with some reserve about the accuracy of the pedigrees.

We are the more inclined to accept the traditional date for the following reasons. In *The Way of the Sea*, p. 135, and again in *Merchant Venturers in Bronze*, pp. 141 and 151, we described some inscribed clay tablets brought back by Hrozny from Boghaz Keui, a village on the Halys river in Asia Minor, the site of the ancient city of Pteria, and before that of Khattussas, the capital of the Hittite Empire. These tablets, which range over many centuries prior to 1200 B.C., are remains of the archives of the Hittite monarchs, and among them is a tablet which is known to date from about 1250 B.C. This tablet related how Dudkhalia III, the Hittite king at that time, had to protect himself from an attack organized by Attarissyas, ruler of Ahhiyava, on his dependency of Zipparla, which has been identified as Caria. Dr. Forrer has transliterated this name, which is rendered T-r-s-y-s in the Hittite script, as Attarissyas, and has identified him as Atreus, ruler of Achaea. Professor Sayce, on the other hand, writes the word Tarsiyas, and identifies him with Perseus or Pterseus. Perseus, however, was ruler in Argolis, and his people are more usually called Argives or Danaans, while Agamemnon, the son of Atreus, was king and leader of the Achaeans. With Myres, then, we agree with Forrer's interpretation, and, if Atreus was living and organizing an attack upon the Hittite empire about 1250 B.C., we cannot expect that his son, Agamemnon, led the Achaean host against Troy much later than 1190 B.C.

After 1200 B.C. an important crisis occurred throughout the

greater part of the Old World. In 1169 B.C. the Kassite Dynasty, which had ruled at Babylon since about 1746 B.C., suddenly came to an end, and, though a new dynasty was founded at that city, the whole country was over-run by Aramaean tribes from the western desert. About 1205 B.C. the death of Merneptah II was accompanied by the fall of the 19th Dynasty in Egypt. After five years of anarchy under a Syrian usurper, the feeble 20th Dynasty followed, and Egypt lost its imperial importance. About 1200 B.C. the Hittite documents suddenly cease, and it is believed that this great empire had come to an end. In 1194 B.C. Troy was destroyed by the Achaeans, and in 1122 B.C. the Shang or Yin Dynasty in China gave way to the Chou Dynasty.

After these crises we witness the rise of the Greeks, the Phoenicians, the Philistines, the Hebrews, and other nations that fill the picture of what is generally known as Ancient History. We propose, therefore, to divide the following chapters of this volume into two parts, dealing first with the decline and fall of the older empires and then with the rise of the later powers.

Before closing the present chapter we must discuss a question that has occupied the attention of many Greek scholars for more than a generation, the origin of the Greek people; or, more accurately speaking, the entry into Greek lands of those tribes with Indo-European speech, who gave to the people of Greece their language and much of their art and religion, and who were the dominant element in the population during the great days of Greece. We have already touched upon the matter in earlier volumes, we have discussed these people as the Hellenes and they are Myres's subject in his book *Who were the Greeks?*

The Greeks themselves recognized three main groups of dialects, the Aeolic, spoken mainly in Thessaly and Boeotia, the Ionic, in Euboea and Attica, and the Doric, which was chiefly used south of the Isthmus of Corinth. To these, modern philologists have added two more; one series spoken in Arcadia,

Cyprus, and the Greek colonies in Pamphylia, usually known as the Arcadian or Cypro-Arcadian, the other the dialects of north-western Greece, which are admitted to be variants, probably primitive variants, of the Doric dialect. This suggests that the

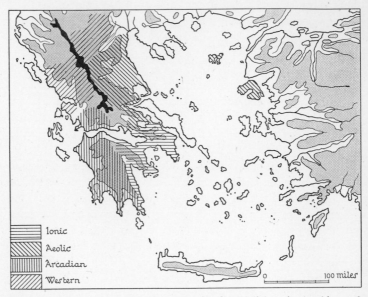

FIG. 1. Map of Greece, showing the distribution of dialects in the thirteenth century (after Myres).

Indo-European invaders arrived in four bands. Greek tradition asserts that the Dorian invasion of the Peloponnese took place at least two generations after the Trojan War, while the intrusion of the Western dialects into Phthiotis, Malis, Locris, and Phocis, driving a wedge between the Aeolic of Thessaly and Boeotia, suggests that they were relatively late invaders.

Arguing from these data, Myres believes that in the thirteenth and twelfth centuries the Aeolic dialects were spoken con-

tinuously from near the mouth of the river Vardar as far south
as Lake Copais in the Boeotian Plain, that Ionic dialects ranged
from there across the Isthmus and spread over the north-
eastern corner of the Peloponnese and down its eastern coast,
while Arcadian was spoken over the rest of the Peloponnese and
to some extent north of the Gulf of Corinth. He thinks the
Ionic dialects the first to arrive, and the Aeolic dialects then
became established in Thessaly and Boeotia; the Arcadian
dialects came early in the fourteenth century, as the Doric did
later, from the north-west across the Gulf of Corinth.

Myres has suggested that the tribes speaking these dialects
entered the Balkan peninsula about 1900 B.C., and that those
speaking Aeolic and Ionic dialects entered Thessaly soon afterwards, and were responsible for the oval houses that appear there
about the time of the foundation of the Second City of Orchomenos. He thinks they were the makers or users of the grey 'Minyan' ware that we have described in some of our earlier volumes.

He has also propounded a very novel view, which we must
discuss here. It will be remembered that in an earlier volume of
this series, *Priests and Kings*, p. 120, we noted that there was
evidence for the arrival of elements of Cycladic culture on the
coast of Argolis; these, which we believed to have been brought
over about 2800 B.C., included certain pottery, covered with a
faint glaze, which we termed primitive glazed ware. We noted,
too, that at a slightly later date this ware had spread northwards
as far as the city of Orchomenos, where it was found in the
second settlement, associated with houses of an oval plan.
Myres has suggested that this primitive glazed ware, which he
calls smear-ware, and the oval houses were brought in from the
north by pastoral people speaking an Indo-European tongue,
who entered Thessaly, perhaps down the Peneus valley or from
Macedonia, about the time of the destruction of Hissarlik II,
and whose passage through Thessaly as far as central Greece is

marked by a number of tumuli, most of which he attributes to this period. These new-comers, he believes, were the first to introduce Indo-European speech into Greek lands, and subsequently became divided into two groups, those remaining in Thessaly speaking Aeolic dialects, while those that passed south, and mixed more with the native population, ultimately developed the Ionic dialects.

This attractive hypothesis raises difficulties. The Third City of Orchomenos was founded about the time of the destruction of Hissarlik II, so the Second City must be some centuries older; moreover, careful exploration has recorded no smear-ware north of that city. The origin of the oval house is obscure, but houses ending in semicircular apses, which may be related to them, have been found at Tiryns, Olympia, and at Korakou near Corinth. It is thus possible that the new style of architecture, like the smear-ware, may have been introduced from the south. Lastly, we feel that it is by no means certain that the tumuli in Thessaly date from the period suggested. Those in Macedonia, so Mr. Heurtley has stated, are all of Hellenistic date.

We have suggested in *The Way of the Sea*, p. 69, a view, originally advanced by Dr. Wace, that the main body of invaders, who introduced Indo-European speech into Greek lands, were those who, about 2300 B.C., introduced a new style of pottery into the area at the head of the Maliac Gulf. These people, we thought, entered the plain down the valley of the Spercheios, but Myres has suggested that they came from a different direction. He has pointed out that similar pottery has been found at Boubasta in the upper valley of the Haliacmon in Macedonia, and he suggests that this ware had a wide range over the west of Thessaly. It may be so, though it is not quite clear that the pottery from the two sites is contemporary. In any case, even if the makers of this ware came from the upper valley of the Haliacmon, their easiest route to the Maliac Gulf would have left the Haliacmon valley at its southern bend for the north-western corner of the Thessalian plain, and, skirting the foot of Pindus, crossed an easy pass into the valley of the Campylus and thence over the pass at the foot of Mt. Tymphrastus to the

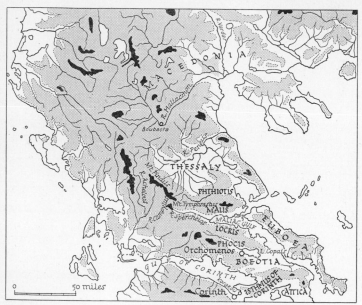

FIG. 2. Map of northern Greece.

Spercheios valley. If, as seems quite possible, the pottery at Boubasta is the later of the two, the original makers of it probably came down the valley of the Achelous, and divided in the Campylus valley, one part crossing to the Spercheios and the other pushing north till they ultimately reached the valley of the Haliacmon.

We are still inclined to think that these new arrivals on the Maliac Gulf were those who first called themselves Hellenes, and were one of the earliest tribes to introduce Indo-European speech into Greek lands. We feel inclined to identify them at any rate with the original speakers of the Ionic dialects.

Whether they were also the ancestors of those of Aeolic speech we do not feel so confident, since there is much to be said for the view that those dialects were brought in by the makers, or rather the users, of the painted pottery, introduced at the beginning of the Second Thessalian period and known as Dhimini ware. It is generally admitted that this ware was brought from the Black Earth lands of the Rumanian plain by refugees whose villages had been destroyed by the Kurgan or Red-ochre people from the Russian steppes. It is possible, however, that the invaders of east Thessaly were none other than the men from the steppes, who spoke, we believe, an Indo-European tongue, and that these steppe-men had carried with them captive women from the Black Earth villages that they had destroyed, and that the Dhimini ware was the work of these captured women, domesticated by their conquerors, for, as Myres reminds us, pot-making is 'woman's work'.

M. Pottier has recently stated his belief that some of the early Hittite pottery shows by its designs that it is related to the Dhimini ware and to that of the Black Earth lands; Myres seems also to support this view. The Hittite invaders were, it is now generally agreed, steppe-men, who had passed through the Black Earth region on their way to Asia Minor. This corroborates, therefore, our suggestion that the invaders of east Thessaly came also from the steppe, and may have been the first to introduce into Greek lands some form of Indo-European speech.

### BOOKS

BURN, A. R. *Minoans, Philistines, and Greeks* 1400–900 B.C. (London, 1930).
MYRES, J. L. *Who were the Greeks?* (Berkeley, 1930).
*Cambridge Ancient History*, vol. ii (Cambridge, 1924).
ROBINSON, T. H. *A History of Israel* (Oxford, 1932).

# 2

# The Near East in the Fourteenth Century B.C.

SIR ARTHUR EVANS suggests that the fall of Minoan power was a consequence of the harsh rule of the lords of Knossos, and of a destructive revolution that this provoked. Glotz thinks that the middle-men of Knossos were cut out when direct trade arose between Egypt and Mycenae. The destruction in Crete seems, however, to have been widespread and complete, which suggests the work of an aggressor from without, and Burn believes that there is much truth in a local tradition still current in the fifth century B.C., and thus summed up by Herodotus.

Minos, the king of Knossos, wished to punish a famous technical expert, Daedalus, who had conspired with the queen against him. Daedalus took to flight, literally, according to tradition, by fixing to his shoulders a pair of wings, and so escaped to Sicily. Minos, having equipped a great fleet, went in pursuit of him, and found him at Kamikos, a Sicanian city to the west of Agrigentum. Here, however, the king came to a violent end. To avenge his death his Cretan subjects set out with another fleet, and besieged Kamikos unsuccessfully for five years, until, for lack of food supplies, they were forced to raise the siege and set sail for home. Rounding the Calabrian promontory, the heel of Italy, a violent storm drove the Cretan fleet upon the rocks, and, as they were unable to return to their island, the survivors went inland and founded the city of Hyria. Crete, being thus denuded of its best fighting men, was left with a diminished population, until other people arrived, chiefly from the mainland of Greece, to take their place.

Diodorus Siculus, writing some centuries later, gives further details of this event, and asserts that, according to Cretan tradition, the body of Minos was taken back to Crete, and buried in a tomb over which was erected a temple or mortuary chapel.

The intercourse between Crete and Sicily is attested by many remains of Minoan civilization discovered in the western island,

FIG. 3. The temple and tomb of Minos.

the presence of Cretan refugees in the Calabrian peninsula seems likely from the survival there to this day of dry built cor-belled chambers, known as *truddhi*, which closely resemble the vaulted tombs of the Mesara plain in Crete. In the spring of 1931 Sir Arthur Evans found a temple, overlying a tomb, of the Second Late Minoan period, in the hill-side immediately south of the Palace of Knossos, and states that this is very like that described by Diodorus. On the other hand, Herodotus states that the death of Minos occurred three generations before the siege of Troy, which would place its date about 1300 B.C.

For some years there had been peace in the Near East, for Amenhotep III, king of Egypt from 1411 to 1375 B.C., had no desire to push Egyptian conquests farther north, and had made friends with Kara-Indash, the Kassite king of Babylon. This alliance kept the Assyrians from threatening the northern frontier of Babylonia, while Amenhotep had purchased peace with the Mitanni in 1401 B.C. by a marriage. The Hittites, under Hattushil, were increasing their power over nearly all Asia Minor, having wrested from the Kharrians the province of Kissuwadna, north of the Taurus mountains.

On the mainland of Greece the richest and most important centre was Mycenae, which then dominated the fertile plain of Argolis, and held the pass between that region and the head of the Gulf of Corinth. This region seems to have been under the rule of the kings who were buried in the shaft graves; these, as we suggested in *Merchant Venturers in Bronze*, p. 108, were probably Hellenes. According to tradition, two fresh sets of people appear to have arrived about this time, Cadmus and his followers at Thebes, and Danaus and his people in Argolis.

All the evidence, traditional and archaeological, points to the arrival of the Cadmeians, apparently from Crete, about the year 1400 B.C.; they introduced into their new home the alphabet, or rather linear syllabary, of Crete, but converted it into a true alphabet in order to enable the illiterate Boeotians to write with it their Hellenic dialect. They were not the first Cretans to settle in this part of central Greece, for some of the remains found in the palace of Thebes go back to the First Late Minoan period. Since the arrival of the Cadmeians so nearly synchronizes with the fall of Knossos, we may suspect that they were refugees, who left Crete after the disaster, and were in no sense responsible for it.

Danaus is said to have been the brother of Aegyptus, with whom he quarrelled; he then left his land with fifty daughters, who had married fifty sons of Aegyptus, and came by sea to the coast of Argolis. Myres has well argued that this signifies that

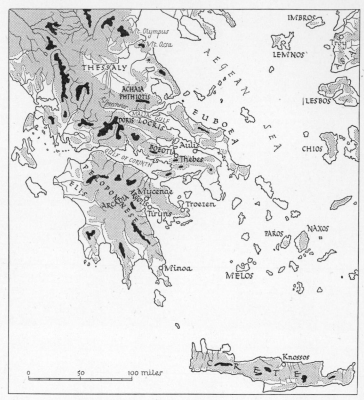

FIG. 4. Map of Greece about 1400 B.C.

Danaus, perhaps the personification of the leader of a band of Danaans, had been serving as captain of a troop of Cretan mercenaries in Egypt, where he had quarrelled with the king and had departed with his troops and their families, including many women who were accompanied by Egyptian husbands. Calculating back the generations from Clytemnestra, one of his descendants, and allowing three generations to the century, Myres would bring the Danaans to Argolis some years before 1400 B.C. On the other hand, he quotes a statement from Manetho, the Egyptian historian, that Danaus was one of the many who tried to usurp the throne after the death of Ikhnaton, and that he was eventually expelled from Egypt by Harmais, who is doubtless Harmhab, who ascended the throne of Egypt in 1346 B.C.

We are inclined to attach more importance to this last statement than Myres appears to do. It often happens, when tracing a line through the eldest son, that the generations are four to the century, and through daughters even five. Thus if Danaus was a man of 65 when he left Egypt in 1346 B.C., and we reckon that each eldest child was born when his father was 25 and his mother 20, a not unreasonable supposition in Mediterranean lands, Iphigenia would have been 12 years of age when she was sacrificed at Aulis. It seems to us, therefore, more probable that the Danaans arrived in Argolis in 1346 B.C., being unwilling to return to Crete after the Minoan power had vanished.

Such was the political condition of surrounding lands, as we interpret the evidence, at the time of the fall of Knossos; we must now discuss the identity of the aggressors. In the fourth century B.C. the Athenian writers told many tales of their great hero Theseus, how he slew the Minotaur and, with the aid of Ariadne, the fair dancing princess, escaped from Crete, abandoned his saviour at Naxos on the homeward voyage, and some years later secretly built a fleet at the desolate harbour of Thymoitadae near Troezen, and successfully raided Knossos. Burn has well pointed out that Philochorus describes how Ariadne fell in love with Theseus when she saw him in the arena, yet for women to be sightseers on such occasions was unthinkable

at Athens in the time of Philochorus, though the frescoes at
Knossos show us that such practices were customary in Late
Minoan Crete. This seems to show that the story was not an
invention of the Classical Age, but that there is a considerable
substratum of truth in this legend of Theseus.

There are still two difficulties in accepting this interpretation
of the events. The first, to which we have already referred, is

FIG. 5.  Bull-leaping fresco at Knossos.

that, according to Herodotus, Minos met his end three generations before the siege of Troy, that is to say about 1300 B.C.,
while the palace was destroyed a century earlier. The other is
that, according to Athenian tradition, Theseus was driven from
Athens by Menestheus, who led the Athenian forces against
Troy.

Mentions of Minos occur frequently in tradition. For instance, there was Minos the great lawgiver and judge, Minos of
the Minotaur and the fatal Sicilian expedition, Minos the son of
Europa and nephew of Cadmus, and Minos the grandfather of
Idomeneus, the leader of the Cretan contingent in the Trojan
War. It is clear that these are not all the same individual, and
even in antiquity it was recognized that there must have been

two, grandfather and grandson. Both of these, however, belong
to a time subsequent to the fall of Knossos. If we are to believe
that the Sicilian expedition led to that catastrophe, we must
postulate more than two of that name. It has been thought by
some that Minos was a name held by more than one king in the
same family. We would go farther and suggest that it was the
title of the king of Knossos, as Pharaoh was a title of the king of
Egypt, and that it was held by the kings of more than one
dynasty. There may well, then, have been four or more kings
known by that name, the lawgiver, the hero of the Sicilian
expedition, the son of Europa, and the grandfather of Idomeneus.
Since a number of sea-ports, both on the mainland of Greece
and on the Aegean islands, are called Minoa, and seem to be
posts connected with the Cretan trade, we feel that their names
must go back to the great days of Cretan commerce that ended
with the fall of Knossos.

The legends of Athenian heroes are curiously involved and
duplicated. Myres considers them most important and trust-
worthy, while Burn attributes them largely to fourth-century
Attic writers, engaged in magnifying the exploits of their
former rulers. The reliable pedigree of the kings of Athens is
relatively short, and goes back only to Cecrops in the latter half
of the fourteenth century. Before that a number of kings are
mentioned, mostly with names similar to those of later occupants
of the throne, but with different and more primitive legends.
This seems best explained by believing that consecutive tradition
went back only to about 1350 B.C., and that there were current
certain tales of earlier but nameless kings. We suspect, however,
that the hero of the Minotaur legend had originally no connexion with Athens, but was a nameless chief of Troezen, whose
exploits were attached by the Athenians to their national hero,
who lived more than 150 years later.

We believe the chief political events of this time, briefly

recapitulated, to have been the establishment of a number of Cretan colonies on the mainland in Middle and Late Minoan times, of which Tiryns, Mycenae, and Thebes were the most important. Then the users of the grey Minyan ware, whom we have ventured to identify with the Hellenic invaders, took these cities from their Cretan lords, and established their rule over central Greece and the eastern half of the Peloponnese, where,

FIG. 6.  Vases of the Third Late Minoan period.

after much mixing with the Cretans and the aborigines, their primitive Hellenic tongue became modified and degenerated into the Ionic dialect. Eventually, owing to unsuccessful naval attacks on Sicily, Crete became denuded of its best fighting men, so that an Ionic ruler of Troezen, who may have been called Theseus, successfully raided Knossos and brought the power of the Cretan nobles to an end. As a result of this the Cadmeians fled from Crete and captured part of Boeotia from its Hellenic rulers, while other Cretans left for the coasts of Asia Minor and Syria, or to take service as mercenaries with the kings of Egypt. After the fall of the 18th Dynasty these failed to make terms with Harmhab, so sailed for Argolis and in time ousted the Ionian rulers of Mycenae.

After the fall of Knossos, Cretan art degenerated, for there were now no rich patrons to support it. The making of fine pottery ceased, and the potters turned out wares by mass production, usually decorated only with lines of colour painted on the lathe. Such other decoration as survived was a meaningless repetition of motives, such as the octopus and the triton shell, now quite conventionalized. The linear script went out of use, and the only new feature was the use of a simple bronze catch-pin for fastening clothes: this, which had no spring, developed later into the simple bow *fibula* or brooch, like the modern safety-pin. As we have seen, the few princes or rich merchants, who survived the fall of Knossos, left for other lands or to take service abroad, and there was a great increase in the broad-headed members of the population, suggesting a number of fresh arrivals from Caria.

FIG. 7. Catch-pin from Crete.

The civilization of the Peloponnese remained much the same, though Mycenae continued to grow in wealth and the whole of Argolis was flourishing under its Hellenic rulers. Its civilization, which is known as Mycenean, was of Cretan origin, but this degenerated too, though not quite so fast as that in Crete. Cretan or Mycenean goods were traded to most parts of Greece and the Aegean islands, and even reached the shores of Asia Minor.

It will be remembered that, according to our view, the Hellenes had arrived some centuries earlier from the mountain region of western Greece down the Spercheios valley to the Maliac Gulf, and that the greater part of these invaders had turned southwards into central Greece, where they had adopted the grey Minyan ware, and had subsequently become masters of the eastern part of the Peloponnese. The more southerly group of these Hellenes had come to speak the Ionic dialect, and we will

now call them Ionians. Those, however, who had remained in
Locris, just south of the Maliac Gulf, together with the tribes
from Doris, in the hill country to the south-west, moved northwards about 1400 B.C., or perhaps a little earlier, into the district
known as Phthia, afterwards Achaia Phthiotis, in the south-east
corner of Thessaly. Here they were, perhaps, joined by some
survivors of those people, who had long before introduced the
Dhimini ware into eastern Thessaly, if, as we have suggested,
these had been Nordic people of Indo-European speech. The
main mass of these people was known shortly afterwards as
Aeolians or Sons of Aeolus, and spoke the Aeolic dialect. The
tribe from Doris, who were known later as the Dorians and spoke
the Doric dialect, settled to the west of them, but were driven
still farther northwards a few years later by the Cadmeians of
Thebes, and settled among the foot-hills of Ossa and Olympus.
A little later, about 1300 B.C., some Hellenic tribes, coming from
the mountain region to the west of Greece, passed southwards
to the Gulf of Corinth; crossing the gulf they occupied the
province of Elis, and before long the greater part of the Peloponnese. These, it is believed, introduced there the Arcadian
dialect.

It will be remembered that in *Merchant Venturers in Bronze*,
p. 111, we mentioned that some people, who we believe to have
been Dardanians, crossed the Hellespont about 1700 B.C. and
built a village on the hill of Hissarlik. This village is known as
Hissarlik V. It seems likely that other groups of Dardanians
occupied the foot-hills around Hissarlik, and in fact the whole of
this corner of the promontory, which became known to the
Egyptians in the time of Thutmose III as *Asy*, a little later to
the Hittites as *As-su-va*, and to the Greeks as *Asia*; other groups
of Dardanians remained in Europe, and were at a later date
settled just north of the Paeonians, in the Morava valley and in
Illyria not far from the Adriatic shore. If we may trust certain

Greek traditions, some of which go back to the seventh century, traders from Crete had settled in the south corner of what was afterwards the Troad. These, who were known later as Teucrians, introduced the name of Mount Ida, and the worship of

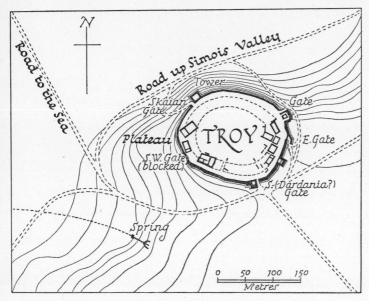

FIG. 8. Plan of Hissarlik VI.

the Sminthian Apollo. Other traditions suggest that at this time there was some intermarriage between the Dardanians and the Teucrians. It was about 1400 B.C., according to Myres, but rather before 1500 B.C. according to Wace, that some of these Dardanians built a well fortified city upon the mound of Hissarlik, known to archaeologists as Hissarlik VI, but to the Hittites a generation later as *Ta-ro-i-sa*, and to the Hellenes as *Troia*.

C 2

Meanwhile the Hittites ruled most of Asia Minor and had a precarious hold on north Syria, and had extended their frontier to the Euphrates at Carchemish. Their supremacy in this region had been threatened by the Kharrian and Mitanni tribes, who occupied the lands around Haran. Shortly before 1400 B.C. the Kharrians had wrested from Hattushil, the Hittite king, the rich province of Kissuwadna, in the valley of the Carmalas, and about 1415 B.C. the Assyrians crossed the Euphrates and raided the provinces near the Taurus range. Hattushil was succeeded about 1400 B.C. by his son Shubbiluliuma, who established his rule firmly throughout Cappadocia, recovered the province of Kissuwadna and eventually that of Arzawa, whose prince, Tarkhundarush, had been carrying on an independent correspondence with the king of Egypt, and had received in marriage one of that monarch's daughters. Shubbiluliuma also claimed to have conquered the Kharrians, and he certainly confined their activities to the eastern side of the Euphrates.

Having consolidated his power, Shubbiluliuma determined to annex those Syrian provinces which had formerly belonged to his predecessors, but were now in the hands of the Mitanni or subject to Egypt. To this end he led an expedition there about 1375 B.C., and, with Kharrian troops as his allies, marched against the Alshe or Alzi, who had taken possession of some of the Mitannian lands, and against Tushratta, king of the Mitanni, and brother-in-law of Amenhotep III, king of Egypt. Though Tushratta was at first successful in withstanding this attack, he was eventually compelled to withdraw to the north-east. His kingdom was ravaged by the Hittite forces, and in the end he became a vassal of Shubbiluliuma and had to break off his friendly relations with Egypt. Soon afterwards Tushratta came to a violent end, and his successor, Mattiuazza, had his kingdom reduced on the west by the Hittites and on the east by the Assyrians. Long before his death, which seems to have occurred

Fig. 9   Chronological chart of the kings in the Near East.

| DATE B.C. | EGYPT | HITTITES | ASSYRIA | BABYLONIA | DATE B.C. |
|---|---|---|---|---|---|
| 1400 | **DYNASTY XVIII**<br>Amenhotep III<br>Amenhotep IV (Ikhnaten)<br>Sakere<br>Tutenkh-amon<br>Harm hab | Shubbiluliuma<br><br>Arnuandash II<br>Murshil II | Ashur-bel-nisheshu<br>Ashur-rim-nisheshu<br>Ashur-nadin-akhi<br>Eriba-Adad<br>Ashur-uballit<br>Enlil-nirari<br>Arik-den-ilu | **KASSITE DYNASTY**<br>Kara-Indash I<br>Kadashman-Enlil<br>Burna-Buriash II<br>Kara-Khardash<br>Kadashman-Kharbe<br>Kurigalzu III<br>Burna-Buriash III<br>Kurigalzu IV | 1400 |
| 1300 | **DYNASTY XIX**<br>Seti I<br>Ramses II | Mutallu<br><br>Hattushil III<br><br>Dudkhalia III | Adad-nirari I<br><br>Shal-maneser I<br><br>Tukulti-Ninurta I | Nazi-Maruttash II<br>Kadashman-Turgu<br>Kadashman-Enlil II<br>Kudur-Enlil<br>Shagarakti-Shuriash<br>Kashtiliash III<br>Enlil-nadin-shum<br>Kadashman-Kharbe II<br>Adad-shum-iddin<br>Adad-shum-nasir | 1300 |
| 1200 | Mernepteh<br>Amen-mose<br>Ramses-Siptah<br>Seti II<br>**DYNASTY XX**<br>Sethnakht<br>Ramses III | Arnuandash IIII<br><br>Dudkhalia IV<br><br>TROJAN WAR | Ashur-nadin-Apli<br>Ashur-nirari III<br>Enlil-kudur-user<br>Ninurta-apal-ekur I<br><br>Ashur-dan I | Meli-Shipak II<br>Marduk-apal-iddin I<br><br>Ilbaba-shum-iddin<br>Enlil-nadin-akhe | 1200 |
| 1100 | Ramses IV<br>Ramses V<br>Ramses VI,VII,VIII<br>Ramses IX<br>Ramses X<br>Ramses XI<br>**DYNASTY XXI**<br>Hrihor<br>Psibkhenno | | Ninurta-tukulti-ashur<br>Mutakkil-nusku<br>Ashur-resh-ishu<br>Tiglath-pileser I<br>Ninurta-apal-ekur<br>Ashur-bel-kala<br>Enlil-rabi<br>Ashur-bel-kala<br>Shamshi-Adad IV | **DYNASTY OF ISIN II**<br>Marduk-shapik-zeri<br>Ninurta-nadin-shum<br>Nebuchadnezzar I<br>Enlil-nadin-apli<br>Marduk-nadin-akhe<br>Itti-marduk-zer-mati<br>Adad-apal-iddin<br>Marduk-akhe-eriba<br>Marduk-zer-.....<br>Nabu-shum-libur | 1100 |
| 1000 | Painozem<br>Menkheperre<br>Amenenopet<br>Siamon | | Ashur-nasir-pal I<br>Shulmanu-asharid<br>Ashur-nirari IV<br>Ashur-rabi II<br>Ashur-resh-ishi II | | 1000 |
| 950 | Hor-Psibkhenno | | Tiglath-pileser II | | 950 |

about 1358 B.C., Shubbiluliuma had conquered the whole of Syria, and he died leaving a large and well consolidated empire to his son, Arnuandash II, at whose death about 1355 B.C. it passed to his brother Murshil II.

Before we proceed to trace the history of Mesopotamia during this eventful half-century, we must pause to examine the cause of the sudden success of Shubbiluliuma and his Hittite forces. Such sudden successes are usually due to some fresh acquisition in the munitions of war, and, as we shall see in Chapter 4, this rise of the Hittite power was no exception to the rule: the new discovery was the use of iron.

Turning to Mesopotamia, we find that just before 1400 B.C. Kara-Indash, the Kassite king of Babylon, and Ashur-bel-nisheshu, the king of Assyria, fearing the aggression of the Egyptian king, whose expeditions had reached to the Euphrates, made an agreement as to their common boundary, and were prepared, if necessary, to meet together any attack from the west, while the Assyrian monarch refortified the citadel at his new town of Ashur. Amenhotep III, however, had no intention of extending his empire beyond the Euphrates, so the Mesopotamian kings made peace with him, while Kadashman-Enlil I, who had succeeded his father Kara-Indash in 1401 B.C., dispatched his sister to be a member of the harem of Amenhotep.

Subsequent events in Mesopotamia were of little interest, and a list of the kings ruling there will be found on p. 21. About 1375 B.C. the Asiatic provinces of Ikhnaton revolted, and Tushratta, the Mitannian king, endeavoured to support the tottering power of Egypt. This was an opportunity too tempting to Shubbiluliuma, who invaded Mitanni and brought most of its land under his control. Then followed a rebellion, in which Tushratta was slain by his son Artatama II. What was left of Mitanni now fell into the hands of the Assyrians; their king, Enlil-nirari, who had succeeded his father Ashur-uballit in

1368 B.C., attacked Babylonia and utterly defeated Kurigalzu III at Susagi on the Tigris. The boundaries between these two kingdoms were now re-adjusted, much to the advantage of the northern power.

Artatama II had, it would appear, welcomed the Assyrian interference in Mitannian affairs, though his action was resented by most of his people. An attempt was made, chiefly by the Kharrians, to put in his place his brother, Mattiuaza, but Shuttarna, Artatama's son, drove his uncle into exile, and sought to please the Assyrians by returning the silver and gold doors that had been carried off many years previously by Shaush-shatar. The Kharrians resented his action and sought the help of Babylon, but the Kassite king of that city, desiring to give no further offence to the Assyrians, promptly seized their property, including two hundred chariots. At this juncture Shubbilu-liuma, anxious to keep on friendly terms with the Mitanni, drove out the Assyrians and the men of Alshe; then he placed Mattiuaza on the throne and gave him his daughter in marriage.

By 1350 B.C. the Asiatic empire of Egypt was a thing of the past, Shubbiluliuma had built up a great dominion, which passed at his death to his son Arnuandash, who held it until 1356 B.C., when he was succeeded by his brother Murshil II. Enlil-nari still held Assyria, while Burna-Buriash III, who had succeeded to the throne of Babylon in 1367 B.C., was able to retain his somewhat diminished kingdom intact.

## BOOKS

BREASTED, J. H.  *A History of Egypt* (New York, 1912).
BURN, A. R.  *Minoans, Philistines and Greeks* (London, 1930).
*Cambridge Ancient History*, vol. ii (Cambridge, 1924).
CHILDE, V. GORDON.  *The Aryans* (London, 1926).
MYRES, J. L.  *Who were the Greeks?* (Berkeley, 1930).

# 3
## The Near East in the Thirteenth Century B.C.

IT will be remembered that in *Merchant Venturers in Bronze*, p. 156, we described how, at the death of Tiy and the old priest Aye, Harmhab, the commander-in-chief of the Egyptian forces, marched on Thebes and ascended the throne as the first king of the 19th Dynasty; this event took place in 1346, or, as some say, in 1350 B.C. Harmhab seems not to have been of royal blood, but a scion of a family that had once been ruling princes of Alabastronpolis. He had commanded the Egyptian army during the reign of Ikhnaton, and seems to have been a most efficient administrator. He put down bribery and extortion with a stern hand, but at the same time raised the salaries of the Civil Servants. He pleased the priests of Ammon by obliterating all evidence of the worship of the Aton and all the monuments of Ikhnaton. He was not in a position to make any attempt to recover the lost possessions in Asia, but he seems to have concluded a treaty with the Hittites. He died, apparently childless, in 1315 or 1321 B.C., and was succeeded by Ramses I, an old man, who planned and began the vast colonnaded hall at Karnak, and then associated his son Seti with himself on the throne. He died in the same or the following year.

Early in his reign Seti I heard that Palestine was being invaded by coalitions of nomad tribes from the desert, and refugees were fleeing to Egypt. Similar letters had been sent by Abdi-Khiba of Jerusalem to Ikhnaton, but had received no attention. Seti pushed on through the frontiers of Canaan and the plain of Megiddo to the Hauran. Then he captured Yenoam, on the southern slopes of Lebanon. After a return to Egypt, he entered Canaan once more and took Kadesh in Galilee. A battle with the Hittites led to the boundary being fixed between Palestine, which was retained by Egypt, and

Syria, which was left in the Hittite empire. For the remainder of his reign he stayed at home, completing the colonnaded hall at Karnak begun by his father, and erecting a number of magnificent buildings at Abydos and elsewhere. This extensive building programme showed signs of exhausting his treasury, so he sent out prospectors to search the eastern desert for gold, which was found in the district of Gebel Zebara and again farther south in the Wadi Alaki; to these mines he established caravan routes, marked at intervals by wells, though the second of these routes had soon afterwards to be abandoned. During his last years his younger son, Ramses, was plotting to remove his elder brother from his path. In this he was successful, for when Seti I died in 1300 or 1292 B.C., he succeeded his father as Ramses II.

We have seen that during the reign of Seti the desert tribes of Transjordania had formed a coalition with a view to the conquest of Palestine, in which they had been in a great measure successful. In these desert tribes many people have recognized the Children of Israel, reaching the Promised Land under the leadership of Joshua. If we may trust the Egyptian accounts of this event, these tribes, though doubtless of the same Semitic speech, were really quite independent of one another until they joined together to cross the Jordan.

West of the Euphrates extended the Hittite empire, now held by Murshil II, brother of Arnuandash, both being sons and heirs of the great organizer Shubbiluliuma. The princes or governors of Carchemish remained faithful, as did Rimisharma, the king of Aleppo, while Murshil signed a treaty with Shunash-shirra, king of Kissuwadna, in which he insisted on the destruction of all the frontier forts. Murshil's chief trouble was with the Amorites of mid-Syria, and it was while endeavouring to subdue these that his army came in contact with that of Seti. The result of the engagement seems to have been that all Syria became included in his empire, while Palestine remained in that of Egypt.

Towards the close of his reign, about 1330 B.C., he found difficulties at the other end of his dominion. It would appear that his rule had extended beyond the mainland on to some of the adjacent islands, and in a document of his time, brought back from Boghaz Keui, it is stated that *La-as-pa* was being attacked by an enemy chief, Tavagalavas, son of Antaravas, who is described as an Ayavalas, and as a ruler of a state called Ahhiyava. Who Tavagalavas was we shall learn later, and it seems unlikely that Murshil was successful in repelling the attack. He died about 1329 B.C., when he was succeeded by his son Mutallu. A few years later the new monarch found himself in difficulties with Seti, who was endeavouring to push the Egyptian frontier farther to the north, and Mutallu made a counter-attack up the valley of the Orontes. This conflict came to a temporary close with the death of Seti, but was renewed, as we shall see, in the time of Ramses II.

We must now return to Tavagalavas, the Ayavalas, the son of Antaravas, who has been identified with good reason with Eteocles the Aeolian, the son of Andreus, who seems to have been considered as the ruler of, or perhaps a ruler in, Achaia, and to have been threatening Lesbos. We saw in our last chapter that the Aeolians had already been growing strong in Phthia, or Achaia Phthiotis, where they had recently arrived from Locris. It would seem that soon after 1350 B.C. one of these Aeolian chiefs, Andreus, went south and conquered the city of Orchomenos, where he founded the settlement known as Orchomenos IV. His son Eteocles seems to have ruled it for a time, since it is said that he introduced there the worship of the Graces. Before long, however, Andreus handed over the city to Athamas, an Aeolian, who held it from him for a time, while Eteocles started expeditions oversea, ravaged the Syrian coast north of the

Orontes, landed in Cyprus and eventually attacked and apparently conquered the island of Lesbos, close to the coast of Asia Minor. About the same time other Aeolians moved still farther south, for Sisyphus settled at Ephyra near Corinth, while Perieres went as far as Laconia.

While this southerly spread of Aeolian chiefs was in progress, the Cadmeians seem to have advanced up the west of Thessaly and then attacked the Dorians, who had been driven by them to the foot-hills of Ossa and Olympus, a district then known as Histiaeotis. The Cadmeians are said by Herodotus to have dislodged the Dorians from this hill-side abode, and to have driven them westward into the foot-hills of the Pindus range. Some of the Dorians, however, according to a tradition preserved by Diodorus Siculus, set out at this time for Crete, where they planted a successful colony. According to Diodorus, they were led by Tectamus, said to be the son of Dorus, who brought them from Thessaly with a mixed assemblage of Pelasgians and Aeolians. Tectamus founded a new kingdom in Crete, which seems to have been derelict and leaderless since the fall of Knossos. He had married a daughter of Cretheus, a son of Aeolus, and by her was the father of Asterius, who succeeded him, and died childless in Crete at a date calculated by Myres to have been about 1300 B.C.

The Danaans, who had settled on the coast of Argolis, seem to have had some trouble with the Egyptian members of their party, and so one night they slew them all. Abas succeeded his grandfather Danaus as chief of the group, and he left two sons, Acrisius, who succeeded him, and Proetus, who took and rebuilt Tiryns soon after 1325 B.C.

No king of Egypt is better known than Ramses II, whose monuments and statues are still to be seen from the north of the Delta to the fourth cataract. Having set aside his elder brother and ascended the throne at a date which is variously stated as

1300 and 1292 B.C., he set to work without delay to complete the monuments started by Seti at Thebes and Abydos, and to give his father a magnificent funeral. In consequence he so exhausted his treasury that he opened up again the track to the gold mines

FIG. 10. Scene from the reliefs of the Battle of Kadesh.

in the Wadi Alaki, which had been abandoned in the time of Seti I. These, however, scarcely provided sufficient for his needs, and he designed a great expedition to recover the Asiatic dominions formerly held by Thutmose III.

In his fourth year he sent an advance army to the Syrian coast to establish a base, where reinforcements could be brought by sea. This base he fixed to the north of modern Beyrout, where a stele of his was found recently. In his fifth year his great army started, by sea and by land, to drive the Hittites out of Syria. His

Egyptian troops were reinforced by Nubian levies and by the Sherden or Shardina, who had been used as a garrison in Syria by Amenhotep III.

Mutallu, the Hittite king, had, as we have seen, fortified his frontier, and when the Egyptian attack was threatened he summoned to his support all his subject peoples and others living on his borders. The kings of Naharin, Arvad, Carchemish, Kode, Kadesh, Nuges, Ekereth, Mesheneth, and Aleppo brought their troops, and contingents came from Kissuwadna and Pidasa or Pedasus. To these were added bands of Lycian sailors, Mysians, Cilicians, who were at this time living south of Mount Ida, Maeonians and the people of Erwenet, a place so far unidentified.

Ramses led his army to the upper waters of the Orontes, over-looking the plain of Kadesh. Learning from some Bedawi that Mutallu and his army had retreated, he made haste to attack the city and fell into an ambush, for the news was false, and his army was completely routed. This disaster, however, was turned into a partial victory by the courage and resourcefulness of the Egyptian king, so that by sunset he was able to leave the field of battle with some justification for claiming a victory, a glorified account of which is depicted on the walls of his temple at Karnak. The result of this campaign, so far from increasing his dominions, nearly led to the complete disappearance of his Asiatic empire, for, at the instigation of the Hittites, all the tribes in Palestine rose in revolt. Ramses thus had to start again to reconquer the territory, and he had re-established his power at the old line, between Palestine and Syria, by the end of the eighth year of his reign. During the next seven years he continued his campaigns, and at the end of the time he had wrested the whole of Syria from the Hittites, and his conquests might have carried him farther had not Mutallu died in 1289 B.C.

Mutallu was succeeded by his brother Hattushil III, who, realizing that his empire was threatened in the west by raids on the part of the Achaeans and in the east by other enemies, took immediate steps to make peace with Egypt. In the twenty-first year of the reign of Ramses, usually computed at 1272 B.C., Hattushil sent messengers to the court of Egypt, bearing a treaty of eighteen clauses, inscribed on a tablet of silver. This treaty, the terms of which had already been agreed by representatives of the two countries, contained a renunciation of hostile attacks in the future on behalf of the two high contracting parties, the re-affirmation of all previous treaties, a defensive alliance, involving assistance of each against the other's foes, and mutual extradition of fugitive offenders. Copies of the treaty were inscribed by Ramses on the walls of two of his temples at Thebes, one of which, that at Karnak, is still in existence; a clay tablet, containing the official Hittite copy, was preserved in their capital, Khattussas, and has been found at Boghaz Keui. In 1259 B.c. the alliance was further cemented by a visit of the Hittite king to the court of Egypt, to celebrate the marriage of his daughter with the Egyptian king. It was probably just before this visit that Ramses had asked Hattushil to send a consignment of iron goods, but had received the reply that at that moment there was none to spare in the warehouses in Kissuwadna. From that time on until the end of his long reign Ramses remained at home building and beautifying the temples of his gods.

We have seen that according to Diodorus Siculus a Dorian colony had been founded in Crete. During the rule of its first leaders Zeus is said to have brought Europa to the island, where their son Minos was born. This story has been considered by many as a myth, and yet it seems probable that, like others of its kind, it is really a legend containing a considerable substratum of truth. The name Europa may give us a clue to its interpretation. The only other occurrence of a similar name is that of the Europus, a river rising in the foot-hills of Olympus and joining the Peneus not far from the base of Ossa. This was the district

into which the Dorians had been driven by the Cadmeians and
from which they were expelled by them about 1325 B.C.  It was
not long afterwards that, according to tradition, Zeus arrived in
Crete with Europa, the sister of Cadmus, or perhaps of some

FIG. 11. Figure, probably of a Hittite king, from the royal gate at Khattussas.

Cadmeian.  It seems possible that soon after the arrival of the
Cadmeians in the valley of the Europus, one of their young
women was carried away by an Aeolian or perhaps Dorian
adventurer and taken to Crete, where their son, on the death of
Asterius, made himself master of Knossos, and took the title of
Minos.  This was the great Minos, who seems to have rebuilt the
Cretan fleet and made the sea-ways safe.  It is also said that he
expelled from the island a number of intruders from Caria,

doubtless the broad-headed people who began to arrive in east
Crete soon after the fall of Knossos. Greek tradition, however,
tended to combine all those known as Minos into one individual.

Acrisius and Proetus seem to have divided between them the
southern part of the plain of Argolis, the former having his
capital at Argos, the latter at Tiryns. The former had an only
daughter, who gave birth to Perseus. This hero seems, like many
others of the time, to have taken to piracy, and to have brought
back a fair princess, Andromeda, from the shores of Palestine.
About 1275 B.C. he took possession of his kingdom of Argos,
which soon afterwards he exchanged for Tiryns with his great-
uncle Proetus; a few years later he drove the Ionians from
Mycenae, which he made the capital of his kingdom, and soon
afterwards many of the Ionians left the Peloponnese, crossed the
Isthmus, and settled in Attica. It was about this time that
Bellerophon, the grandson of Sisyphus, left Ephyra and took
refuge with Proetus, who seems to have been then living at
Argos; owing to domestic difficulties, he had to leave this asylum
and crossed over to Lycia.

It was soon after 1300 B.C. that another movement of peoples
took place; some of the Phrygians, a mountain tribe living near
the Sea of Marmora, crossed the Hellespont and settled on the
slopes of the mountains. Others remained behind in Europe, and
in later days were known as Bryges in the mountains of Macedonia. Some of those settled in Asia Minor were known as
Moschi or Muski. About 1260 B.C. a Phrygian chief, Laomedon,
seized the city of Troy on the mound of Hissarlik, and with the
aid of craftsmen from Crete or the other islands rebuilt its
citadel, which was known as Ilion. A few years later his eldest
son, Priam, as a young man, joined some Phrygian bands who
were repulsing an attack by the Amazons, believed by some to
have been the Hittites.

About the same time certain foreign adventurers appeared in

Greece. Myres has pointed out, as Ridgeway had done before, that the heroes of the Trojan War were either descendants of Aeolus, with fairly long pedigrees, or were grandsons, in some cases great-grandsons, of Zeus or some other god. Thus Achilles and Ajax were grandsons of Aeacus, the son of Zeus, Odysseus was grandson of Arcesius, the son of Zeus, Laodamas was grandson of Nausithous, the son of Poseidon, Diomedes was grandson of Oeneus, the grandson of Ares, while Agamemnon and Menelaus were grandsons of Pelops, the grandson of Zeus. Myres has argued from this that the grandfathers of these heroes had at the same time entered the country from elsewhere, and were in most cases ignorant of their fathers. Who they were and whence they came is not explained by tradition, except in the case of Pelops, who is said to have been a Phrygian. Since the arrival of these god-born heroes from nowhere almost coincides with the arrival of the Phrygians in Asia Minor, Myres has suggested, with great probability, that they were members of this or some allied tribe.

It was, then, about 1260 B.C., or perhaps in some cases earlier, that Aeacus arrived in Aegina, Arcesius in Ithaca, Nausithous in Phaeacia, Oeneus at Pleuron in Aetolia, and Pelops in Elis, where he slew Oenomaus, king of Pisa, and married his daughter Hippodamia. Thus by 1250 B.C. the greater part of Greece and the surrounding islands was under the rule of Aeolians or divine-born heroes of Phrygian origin; in Argolis only and around Thebes were Danaans and Cadmeians able to carry on the Cretan tradition.

Ramses lived to a great age. He celebrated a jubilee in the thirtieth year of his reign and repeated this ceremony every three years. He outlived his eldest twelve sons, and in his old age the coasts of the Delta were ravaged with impunity by the Libyans and a number of oversea pirates allied to them, including the Shardana, the Lycians, and people from the Aegean. At length, having reigned for sixty-seven years, he died in 1233 or 1225 B.C., and was succeeded by Merneptah, his thirteenth son, already an old man.

In the first years of the new king's reign the attacks on the Delta continued, and Merneptah suspected that the Hittite king, Dudkhalia, who had succeeded Hattushil about 1255 B.C., was being false to the treaty concluded between their fathers forty-six years before. Suspicion developed almost into certainty when, in his third year, all his Asiatic subjects rose in revolt from the frontier as far south as Askalon. Merneptah, in spite of his age, led an army against his offending subjects, and managed to quell the revolt. All the rebellious people were severely punished, and among them the Children of Israel, who are here first mentioned by name in the Egyptian records. Then Mery-ey, the king of the Libyans, led a formidable attack upon the Delta, and with him came the Sherden, the Shekelesh, the Ekwesh, the Lykki, and the Teresh, who have been identified with people from near Sardis, from Sicily or Sagalassus, the Achaeans, the Lycians, and the Tyrsenians, who appear later as Etruscans. These people arrived in the Delta early in the fifth year of Merneptah's reign, and were met by the king at the head of the Egyptian army near the royal house of Perire on 15th April, when after a six hours' battle the invaders were defeated and put to flight. Mery-ey escaped when he saw the battle going against him, and, successfully eluding the frontier guards, returned to Libya, where his subjects dethroned him for having led them to disaster.

After this victory Merneptah lived for another five years and died in 1223 or 1215 B.C. At his death two claimants arose for the throne. One of these, Amen-mose, held the kingdom for a short time, when he was supplanted by his rival, Ramses-Siptah, who married Tewosret, generally thought to have been a royal princess. He reigned for about six years, when he was superseded by Seti II, who had been viceroy of Nubia with the title of 'Governor of the Gold Country of Amon'.

Seti II ascended the throne in 1214 or 1209 B.C., but was unable to hold it for long. The nobles and the priests resented his usurpation, and in 1210 or 1205 B.C. he was removed and for a while the land was in a state of anarchy. One interesting souvenir of this king has been found, namely a bronze leaf-shaped sword, of a type more usual in Hungary and central Europe, though occasionally found in the Aegean region, and bearing Seti's cartouche; evidently this was loot taken from some fallen

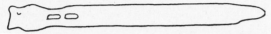

FIG. 12.   Bronze sword, bearing the cartouche of Seti II.

Achaean warrior during the repulse of the allied forces in the Delta in the reign of Merneptah.

For five years there was no settled rule, except that a Syrian adventurer for a time set himself upon the throne. The Libyans again overran the Delta, and there was chaos in the land until in 1205 or 1200 B.C. Setnakht, a man of uncertain origin, but probably a descendant of Seti I, subdued his rivals and ascended the throne as the first king of the 20th Dynasty.

Hattushil III had been succeeded in 1255 B.C. by Dudkhalia III as king of the Hittites, and before many years were past the new king had to defend his lands against an invader from the west. This was an attack organized by Atreus, son of Pelops, king of Elis. Atreus seems to have been a headstrong young man, and with his brother Thyestes had murdered their half-brother Chrysippus. They fled from Elis and took refuge at Mycenae, where the aged Perseus was probably still king. Atreus seems to have taken to a life of piracy, and led marauding bands of Achaeans to attack the Hittite coast. We know little more about the reign of Dudkhalia than has already been given above, except that at his death, about 1229 B.C., he was succeeded by his son Arnuandash III, of whom we know less. He again was succeeded by his son, Dudkhalia IV, about 1200 B.C., when the Hittite records come to an end, and the empire seems to have fallen before a great movement of Phrygian and allied tribes that swept across Asia Minor from the north-west.

All this time Troy, under its Phrygian kings, Laomedon and Priam, had remained independent of the Hittite empire. We gather from the archaeological remains found on the site, in the layer known as Hissarlik VI, that it was remarkably prosperous, and we learn from Hittite sources that there was a district in the north-west of Asia Minor, not under their rule, known to them as *As-su-v-a* or Asia, in which was a city called *Ta-ro-i-sa* or Troia, and that near it was a place by the name of *La-as-pa* or Lesbos.

Atreus seems at this time to have been the most prominent of the unruly Achaeans, who were supporting themselves by a piratical life on the sea, but others were doubtless engaged in similar exploits. It must have been soon after 1250 B.C. that Bellerophon, who had left Argolis for Lycia a few years earlier, was engaged in a war with the Solymi in the interior of the peninsula. The attacks of Atreus upon the Hittite coast became so frequent that about 1230 B.C. Dudkhalia III decided to form an alliance with him, and granted to him and his associate Biggaia the titles of *kurvanas* or *koiranos*, the equivalent of *tyrannos*. A few years later, about 1225 B.C., Atreus made an attack upon Alasya or Cyprus, and, as at this time the Minoan civilization came to an abrupt end in that island, it seems likely that he turned out those of Cretan descent and put in their place a number of Achaeans from the eastern Peloponnese, who introduced the Arcadian dialect, which was spoken there in much later days; but some believe that this settlement was not effected until 1196 B.C.

We must now trace the fortunes of the two Cretan communities, those in Argolis and Thebes, as far as these can be determined by tradition. Perseus, as we have seen, had established himself at Mycenae about 1270 B.C., and ruled there probably until about 1235 B.C., when he was succeeded by his eldest son, Electryon. He had several sons, all of whom were killed by a native chief, Pterelaus of Taphos, and an only daughter, Alcmene, who married Amphitryon, son of Alcaeus, a man of unknown origin. On the death of Electryon, about 1225 B.C., the kingdom passed to his brother Sthenelos, who seems to have died a few years later, leaving a son Eurystheus, probably a boy at the time. Atreus, who had during all his wanderings kept Mycenae as a base, seems to have ousted the young Eurystheus and established himself at Mycenae. As a young man, Atreus is said to have married Cleola, by whom he had a son Pleisthenes, who married Aerope, daughter of Minos of Knossos. Later on Pleisthenes died, and Atreus was a widower, so he took Aerope as his second wife, and by her became the father of Agamemnon and Menelaus. In the meantime Alcmene had given birth to twin sons, Heracles and Iphicles, and the former of these was a claimant to the throne of Mycenae.

Cadmus had married Harmonia, according to tradition a daughter of Ares, and therefore presumably of Hellenic descent. By her he had four daughters, Agave, Autonoë, Ino, and Semele, and one son, Polydorus, apparently much younger than his sisters. Agave married Echion, one of the original band of Cadmeians, and, after the death or retirement of Cadmus, their son Pentheus became king to the exclusion of his uncle Polydorus. During his rule his mother and aunts became subject to attacks of religious frenzy, and held orgies on Mount Cithaeron; similar frenzies are recorded at later dates from south-west Asia. Pentheus tried in vain to check these extravagances, and climbed into a tree to watch them. Here he was detected by the enthusiasts, who, mistaking him for a wild beast, tore him in pieces. Autonöe married Aristaeus, by whom she became the mother of Actaeon, who was torn to pieces by his hounds. Ino married Athamas, the Aeolian king of Orchomenos, who was by

FIG. 13. Figures of frenzied women dancing. From Knossos.

her the father of Learchis and Melicertes, and then became insane; meanwhile Semele died in giving birth to a new religion.

After the death of Pentheus, Polydorus succeeded to the kingdom, but he died shortly afterwards, leaving it to his son, Labdacus, still a boy. Labdacus died young, leaving an infant son, Laius, to succeed him, and he by his wife, Jocasta, was the

father of Oedipus. The story of the latter's unwittingly in-
cestuous marriage is well known, and, having blinded himself
and abdicated in a fit of remorse, he was succeeded by his sons,
Eteocles and Polynices. These attempted to rule jointly, but,
owing to a dispute, Polynices fled and took refuge at the court of
Adrastus, who was now king of Argos.

We must now follow the fortunes of the family of Proetus,
whom we left at Argos, after he had exchanged Tiryns for it
with Perseus. Proetus seems to have had a son, Megapenthes,
who appears to have died young in his father's lifetime, leaving
him with three daughters, who, like the daughters of Cadmus,
were given to religious frenzies. The old king was so disturbed at
this that he offered his kingdom to any one who would cure
them. There arrived one day two brothers, Melampus and Bias,
sons of Amythaon, an Aeolian physician. They professed to have
effected a cure, married two of the daughters and inherited
between them the kingdom of Argos. Bias was succeeded by his
son, Talaus, who married Lysimache, and it was in the house of
their eldest son, Adrastus, who succeeded in due course to the
kingdom, that Polynices took refuge after his flight from Thebes.
For a time Adrastus was expelled from Argos, and became king of
Sicyon, but soon afterwards he recovered his former kingdom.
Along with Polynices and other heroes he attacked Thebes and
destroyed the Cadmeian power. This, however, was the end also
of the Cretan power in Argolis, for the forces of Argos were so
weakened, that after many struggles Atreus, or at any rate
Agamemnon, brought the whole of Argolis under his rule.
About this time many of the leading men of Cretan extraction
left and settled in Asia Minor, for Amphilochus of Argos,
Chalcas of Mycenae, and Mopsus of Thebes founded cities in
Cilicia.

Thus do the stories handed down by Greek tradition, reinforced by contemporary documents from Egypt and the Hittite

archives, and the results of much archaeological research, set the stage for the enactment of that great tragedy, immortalized by Homer, the Siege of Troy.

## BOOKS

BREASTED, J. H. *A History of Egypt* (New York, 1912).
BURN, A. R. *Minoans, Philistines, and Greeks* (London, 1930).
*Cambridge Ancient History*, vol. ii (Cambridge, 1924).
CHILDE, V. GORDON. *The Aryans* (London, 1926).
MYRES, J. L. *Who were the Greeks?* (Berkeley, 1930).
ROBINSON, T. H. *A History of Israel* (Oxford, 1932).

# 4

# *The Tale of Troy*

THE story of the siege of Troy has often been told. Homer gives vivid descriptions of the combats between the contending heroes; the Greek dramatists relate the story of the Achaean fleet at Aulis and the fate that awaited returning chiefs; while Virgil, probably deriving some of his material from folk memory, gives further details and describes the capture of the city. Since then volumes dealing with this episode have appeared in vast numbers, till it might be thought that nothing remained to be said. We do not propose to tell again this much-told tale, but to endeavour, in the light of the latest information available, to place it in its true setting as part of the history of the time.

We have already seen that a band of Phrygians, hailing ultimately from the Russian steppes, had made themselves masters of the north-western corner of Asia Minor, and had rebuilt the city upon the mound of Hissarlik, which is thenceforward known as Troy. We have also seen reason to believe that a part of this original band had remained behind on the European side of the straits in Thrace, whence some had passed south-westwards to make themselves masters of many of the cities of Greece. These rovers had joined with others of their kind, who had reached Greek lands at an earlier time, to form the great confederacy of the Achaeans, who had for a time been under the leadership of Atreus. How that leadership passed we learn from Homer. When describing Agamemnon's sceptre, 'that Hephaistos had wrought curiously', he tells us that 'Hephaistos gave it to King Zeus son of Kronos, and then Zeus gave it to the messenger-god the slayer of Argus; and King Hermes gave it to Pelops the charioteer, and Pelops again gave it to Atreus shepherd of the host, and Atreus dying left it to Thyestes rich in flocks, and Thyestes in his turn left it to Agamemnon to bear, that over many islands and all Argos he should be lord.' In this way, then, the lordship over the Achaean confederacy, first held by Pelops, and afterwards recognized as the right of Atreus by the Hittite king, passed in due course to Agamemnon, the acknowledged leader of the Achaeans against Troy.

The territories that in some way owed allegiance to Agamemnon are enumerated in the Homeric catalogue of ships. By many this has been considered an interpolation, but, as Myres has shown, the list is in keeping with what we know of Achaean power at that time from other sources. These territories included the whole of the Peloponnese and all the eastern parts of the mainland of Greece as far as the northern boundary of Thessaly, except some few outlying portions of that district. On the other hand the western half of the mainland north of the Gulf of Corinth contributed no contingents, except Aetolia and Dodona with its adjacent region. Doris and southern Locris, on the Gulf of Corinth, were also outside the confederacy. Besides the mainland and the adjacent isles, Euboea, Salamis, Aegina, and the Ionian Isles, a number of more distant islands sent ships and troops against Troy, and so must be considered as forming part of the Achaean group. These were Crete, or that part of it known as the land of a hundred cities, Rhodes, Cos with Calydnae, Nisyrus, Carpathus, and Casus, and the little island of Syme close to the coast of Asia Minor. It will be noticed that these islands all lie to the south of the Aegean region, and most of them in its south-east corner. This is not surprising when we remember that about 1220 B.C. Attarissayas, ruler of the Ahhiyava, whom we believe to be identical with Atreus, ruler of the Achaeans, was attacking Zipparla, which is thought to be Caria, apparently from a base that he had established in Pamphylia, on the south coast of Asia Minor. It can scarcely be a mere coincidence that remains of Mycenean civilization have been found in all the territories enumerated above and are absent from the other regions on the mainland.

The position of Agamemnon has also been the subject of considerable difference of opinion. Leaf believed that, as the contributor of the largest of the combined forces, Agamemnon had been elected by the other kings to the chief command. Bury said that to speak of him as the ruler of a Mycenean 'empire' would perhaps be an overstatement, since no one outside his own kingdom paid him tribute or owed him military service. This may literally be true, though it must be admitted that our information on these points is scanty, but from the passages quoted from the *Iliad* and from a Hittite tablet it is clear that he had inherited a sceptre, the symbol of some definite authority, from Atreus, who had been recognized by the Hittite king as *koiranos*, perhaps the equivalent of *tyrannos*, of the Achaeans. It seems clear from this that he held no ephemeral authority.

According to Leaf, who considered the catalogue a later addition to the poem and of Boeotian origin, Agamemnon was the actual king of the greater part of the mainland, ruling most of the territory within a hundred miles of Mycenae. Beyond this he recognizes only the kingdom of Nestor in Elis, with its capital at Pylos, the kingdom of Peleus in Phthia in southern Thessaly,

FIG. 14. The water tower at Troy.

and that of Odysseus in the Ionian Isles. The catalogue, however, notes many more kingdoms, though some of these may have been vassal states, and a number of Boeotian cities that sent contingents, though these were apparently not under the leadership of Achaean chiefs.

The forces that assisted Priam in the defence of Troy are better known, for the authenticity of the Trojan catalogue, as given in the *Iliad*, has not been disputed. These include all the peoples of the Troad, then the tribes, allied to the original Phrygians, living in Thrace and the adjoining regions to the north of the Aegean Sea, as far west as the Axius or Vardar. Then there were the peoples from the north coast of Asia Minor as far east as Alybe, the birthplace of silver, which is believed to be the Halys valley. Lastly there were the inhabitants of the east coast of the Aegean Sea, the Mysians, the Phrygians, the Maeonians in what was later to be called Lydia, the Carians, and the Lycians as far as the Xanthus river. Thus, if we look upon the Aegean region and the lands abutting on it as a rectangle, Agamemnon commanded all the peoples on the western and southern sides, while those on the north and east owed allegiance to Priam, and a line drawn from the north-western to the south-eastern corner separated the Achaean from the Phrygian world.

We must now discuss the causes that led to this great war between two groups of allied peoples. The traditional cause is, of course, the capture of Helen, the wife of Menelaus, by Paris, the son of Priam, and the refusal of the Trojans to send her back to her husband at Sparta. Few modern students would accept the absolute truth of this story or suppose that it was the sole cause of the Trojan War. It is, of course, possible that raids across the Aegean took place, and the capture of maidens by these piratical chiefs is not unlikely, and more than one such capture is recorded in the *Iliad*. Still such a seizure of a woman even if it were one of a series, would scarcely precipitate such

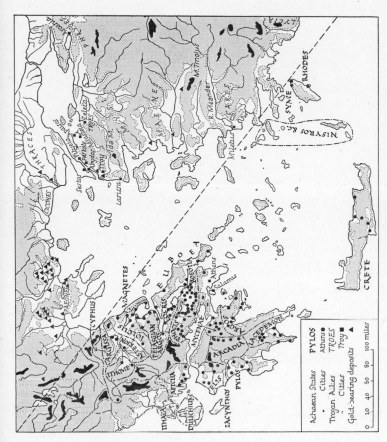

Fig. 15. Map of the Aegean region at the time of the Trojan War.

a war unless one or both sides were prepared for it. Most conflicts have an economic cause, and personal events, such as the seizure of a woman or the murder of a chief, are but pretexts for the declaration of a war long contemplated.

We may, then, search for an economic origin for the Trojan War. Leaf has suggested that the city of Troy, placed conveniently near the straits of the Hellespont, the passage through which is made difficult by dangerous currents, was utilized by its possessors to control the maritime traffic passing from the Aegean to the Euxine. This is likely enough, for its position near the entrance to a narrow strait is comparable to that of Mycenae, at the mouth of the pass leading from the Argolid plain to the Gulf and Isthmus of Corinth. Another valuable asset of the site was that it was an important station on the land route between Asia and Europe, which could most easily cross the dividing straits near this spot. It seems likely, then, that the Trojans had been refusing permission to the Achaeans to pass these straits or had been demanding excessive tolls for the privilege.

Bury is inclined to dismiss this explanation, believing that it is bound up with the hypothesis of an annual fair on the plain of Troy, for which there is no evidence. He seeks for a cause in the desire of the Achaeans to effect settlements on the coast of Asia Minor. Leaf, though he suggested that the plain of Troy was a place where Aegean traders met those from the Euxine, did not rest his argument upon this suggestion; he has given another reason for the desire of the Achaeans to camp on the plain, and this reason seems adequate. The explanation offered by Bury seems to fail, since none of the Achaeans settled at Troy after it was captured, but left it, according to most accounts, in the hands of Aeneas, whose family held it until it was taken from them about the close of the century.

We will return to Leaf's explanation. He points out that

ancient voyagers travelled only by day, and at night beached their boats at some convenient spot, where a good supply of fresh water was obtainable, since their limited space permitted them to ship only a small quantity. He has shown, too, that owing to the nature of the currents, entry into the straits of the Hellespont is a difficult task that would occupy a whole day, so that it was necessary to camp for the night at the first spot within them where ships could be beached and fresh water obtained. The plain of Troy and the Scamander river alone provide these essentials. If the Achaean voyagers were unable to make use of these advantages, the Propontis and the Euxine were barred to them. That a relatively small force is able to bar these straits was made very evident by the campaign at Gallipoli in 1915–16.

Still the barring of the straits would be of little importance unless the Achaeans very much desired to pass them, and we have to seek for a reason sufficient to induce them to undertake a strenuous campaign to free them. Leaf, remembering the importance of the Greek colonies in south Russia in later centuries, suggested that the Achaeans desired to enter the Euxine to obtain corn from the rich lands to the north of that sea. This, however, seems to us unlikely, for it is only when cities have grown so large as to be incapable of feeding themselves with home-grown supplies that they attempt to bring such bulky cargoes from a considerable distance. It is very doubtful whether any city in Mycenean Greece, or, for that matter, in later Greece before the sixth century B.C., had grown to such dimensions that it needed to import grain from a distance. To account for the eager desire of the Achaeans to pass the straits we must search for another motive.

We have seen in an earlier volume of this series, *Priests and Kings*, that objects of Cycladic workmanship had found their way to the south Russian plain perhaps as early as 2600 B.C., and in the *Iliad* itself we have more than one reference to the voyage of the Argonauts, which seems to have passed this way. It is true that the only full account of this voyage is late, and that in consequence many of the details given are suspect, but we have a number of early references to the expedition, which sailed, among other places, to Colchis, on the Transcaucasian coast of the Euxine, in search of the Golden Fleece. This voyage was doubtless in the main a voyage of discovery, and the heroes may have been engaged in commerce or piracy, but the Golden Fleece gives a hint as to its chief object. It was pointed out many years ago that in working alluvial gold deposits, if the dust-laden water were made to flow over a sheep's fleece, much of the metal would be deposited on the surface, from which it could be extracted later, and it was suggested that the voyage of the *Argo* was in search of a gold-field. Whether this gold-field actually existed at Colchis, where the Golden Fleece was sought, is uncertain, but a voyage to the Euxine and up the Lower Danube would bring the adventurers close to Transylvania, where most of the gold of the ancient world was obtained.

Many years ago Myres pointed out that if we divide the Aegean region by a diagonal line from the north-west to the south-east, we should not only divide the Achaean forces from those of the Phrygians, as we pointed out in a previous page, but should also divide the region into two parts, in one of which, the Phrygian, lie all the deposits of gold known in these parts, while in the Achaean half there are none. Though he has made no reference to this fact in his recent work, we believe it to be significant. In earlier days Mycenae was rich in gold, whether derived from Transylvania or perhaps even from Ireland. In its latest phase gold seems to have become scarce, and we can only conjecture that for some reason the supply had been cut off. How and why this occurred is not clear, but it seems likely that the trade-routes between Transylvania and the Peloponnese had been intercepted by the people of the Lausitz culture, to be described in a later chapter, who had already begun their south-eastward movement, which was to land them on the Asiatic coast of the Hellespont within a century of the destruction of Troy. It was, then, we believe, a search for gold, in Transylvania or elsewhere, that caused in the Achaeans the desire to enter the Hellespont; and it was the wish of the Phrygians, who already possessed a monopoly of the local gold-fields, to prevent their rivals from achieving this end. Thus, as so often happens, the accumulation of gold in the treasury of one people, and its scarcity in the coffers of another, led to a state of political friction that ended in a serious war.

Before considering the effects of this war, we must pause to review the civilization of the Achaeans at that time. In the *Odyssey* Homer gives a vivid picture of the house of Odysseus, and the excavations at Mycenae, Tiryns, Athens, and elsewhere have laid bare the foundations of houses of the same type. These houses consisted of a single long living-room, or a series of detached buildings, separated from one another by narrow passages. This type of building, known as a *megaron*, was universally in use on the mainland of Greece during most of the Mycenean period, and has been met with at Hissarlik as early as the Second City, while it occurs, as was seen in an earlier volume, in some of the villages on the Black Earth lands. The *megaron* was always rectangular, it had a fixed central hearth, while its two longer sides were continued at one end to form a porch, from which a single central door led into the room. The porch opened on to a courtyard, surrounded by a pillared cloister. Myres has pointed out why these buildings were separated from one another. He has shown that they were covered with a hip-roof, draining on all four sides, and that provision had to be made for the drip from the eaves of all these. He also suggests that the roof had a clerestory or louvre, to let out the smoke from the central hearth. This style of architecture

clearly originated in a timber structure, which had been converted into stone in the Peloponnese during Mycenean times,

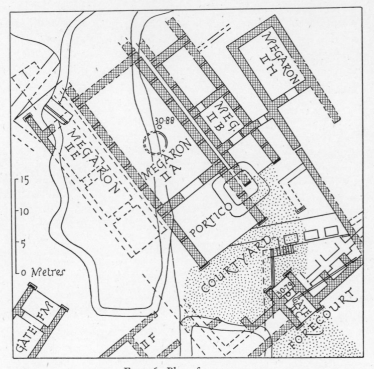

FIG. 16. Plan of a megaron.

though doubtless wooden buildings of this type survived elsewhere; it seems also probable that this style of building arose in
a country with a heavy rainfall.

Where the *megaron* style of architecture began is still uncertain. Myres suggests the western side of the Balkan peninsula,
pointing out that similar hip-roofs occur to-day in Bosnia and

Montenegro. If the Greek temples in their earlier forms go back, as seems likely, to the same originals, one could trace the *megaron* back to wooden houses of the log-cabin type, such as seem to have occurred early in Switzerland, and from which the modern Swiss chalet is derived. On the other hand, it was in use in the Second City of Hissarlik, and in one of the latest villages at Erösd. It appears that it was derived from some primitive log or wooden building that had a wide distribution in the mountain regions of Europe and Asia Minor at a very early date.

The Achaean leaders seem to have been big men, strong and very adventurous. Though sometimes they engaged in overseas trade, they were more prone to piracy and war. In this they closely resemble the Vikings of 2,000 years later. They were evidently only a ruling caste in Greece, and themselves led in the fight, but there was clearly a large population under their rule, which supplied the rank and file of their armies. These are seldom mentioned in the *Iliad*, which is content to record the acts of prowess of the Achaean chiefs, but we gather from one episode that some, at least, of the rank and file were not so enamoured of fighting, and it is significant that their spokesman, Thersites, is described as having a head like a sugar-loaf, which points him out as being a member of the Anatolian-Dinaric variety of the Alpine race. The Achaeans were great trencher-men, and delighted in eating enormous quantities of beef, and offering still larger quantities in the hecatombs that they sacrificed to their gods. Fish they seem never to have touched, and 'fish-eaters' was among them a term of contempt, applied, apparently, to their subject peoples and others whose civilization they despised. This beef-eating propensity seems a further proof, if one were needed, that their ancestors had come originally from the grass-lands of Russia, a view that is further supported by their use of the horse. This they drove in a war chariot, like so many of the early peoples of similar origin, and they do not seem to have ridden on horseback, probably because, like Rolf the Ganger in a later time, they were too big and too heavy to mount the small mountain ponies, the only beasts in their possession.

Fig. 17. A war chariot at Mycenae.

Of the women's dress at this time we know little, except that it was a long tubular garment, fastened down the breast with some kind of clasp. The men, when not arrayed for battle, wore a close-fitting vest or jersey, over which they threw a woollen plaid. Their equipment for battle was varied. Some used an enormous shield of flexible leather, made more rigid by a bronze rim; this was attached over the left shoulder so as to hang before the body, leaving both arms free to use a great thrusting spear.

Sometimes the warriors carried two lighter spears, and, when these had been cast, rushed in with bronze swords, sometimes the long thrusting dirk and at others the leaf-shaped slashing sword. Other warriors were clad in bronze helmets and greaves, carrying on their left arms round parrying shields; these used a single thrusting spear. In other cases the men wore body armour of padded linen covered with bronze plates. It is clear that the battle equipment was as varied as the origin of the men who wore it, and had not yet become standardized. One thing, however, is undoubted: the great majority of the arms used were of bronze, and the use of iron, which had been known for nearly two centuries among the Hittites, had not become general. Iron tools, it is true, were in use among the farmers, and we read of iron knives and axes; for weapons, iron was used only for arrow-heads and in one instance for a mace. Iron swords seem quite unknown to both sets of combatants. Their dead were burned and the ashes laid under a large barrow, a custom that had only recently been introduced, probably by the Phrygians.

Here we may well digress for a moment to sum up what little is known as to the origin of the use of iron. This metal had for long been known in its meteoric state, and occasionally worked, but, since this form of iron is soft and spongy, its use had been confined to ornaments, such as the beads found by Wainwright in a predynastic tomb in Egypt, or for other similar purposes, like the fragments found by Woolley in an early deposit at Ur.

As we mentioned in our last volume, *Merchant Venturers in Bronze*, the earliest known object of true iron, perhaps of steel, is the blade of the dagger found in the tomb of Tut-enkh-amon, which dates from about 1350 B.C. About the same time iron appears as a scarce product at Gerar in Palestine. Less than a century later, at any rate before 1255 B.C., Ramses II of Egypt wrote to Hattushil, king of the Hittites, asking for a supply of iron goods. These Hattushil was unable to supply, as there were none at the moment at Kissuwadna. It seems clear from this that as late as 1250 B.C. the Hittites had the monopoly in iron, though articles of this metal had been traded as far south as Gerar and had reached Egypt a century earlier. Some have thought that Kissuwadna was the centre of this industry, others that this place

was a depot, whence iron could be shipped to the south. There is no evidence, however, that suitable iron ore is to be found in this district, which lies some way from the south coast of Asia Minor, and was not, therefore, a suitable base for the southern trade. It seems more likely that the king of the Hittites was, at the time that the appeal from Ramses arrived, organizing this troublesome province, and, having no surplus stores of iron goods at hand, was not going to take the trouble to have them sent from some other part of his dominions to please a king who might at any time become his rival.

FIG. 18. Warlike equipment of the Achaeans.

Some years ago Professor Gowland, in a most valuable paper on the origin of metallurgy, pointed out that there were only two regions in western Asia where suitable iron ore was to be found, and that only one of these was likely to have been the site of the earliest iron industry, since 'from a metallurgical point of view, deduced from the extent and character of the ancient remains, there are strong reasons for believing that the first-mentioned region was the first in which the metal was regularly produced'. This region he describes as 'on the south-east of the Euxine (ancient Paphlagonia and Pontus) extending from the modern Yeshil Irmak to Batum, and comprising a series of mountain ranges, not far from the coast, along the lower slopes and foot-hills of which the iron deposits are scattered'. The western part of this mountain range is cut through by the river Halys, and about seventy miles south of this range stood the Hittite capital, known then as Khattussas, later as Pteria, and now as Boghaz Keui.

The Greeks used a foreign word, *chalybs*, for steel, to distinguish it from iron, probably meteoric iron, which they called *sideros*. This word *chalybs* is suggestive of the Chalybes, a tribe living later near the Euxine coast a little to the east of Paphlagonia, and believed to be identical with the Alybe country, mentioned by Homer, which also lay in the same direction. It has been thought that Alybe and Chalybes are the equivalent of Khale-wa, the people of the Halys valley. It seems almost certain, then, that it was where the Halys river passes through these iron-stone mountains, at the north of the original territory of the Hittites, that there was first discovered a method of working iron into a form suitable for weapons. It seems almost equally sure that this method must have consisted in smelting the iron with charcoal, thereby producing some form of steel. The date of this discovery is uncertain, but we may conjecture that it was not long before or after 1400 B.C.

### BOOKS

BURN, A. R. *Minoans, Philistines, and Greeks* (London, 1930).
LEAF, W. *Troy. A Study in Homeric Geography* (London, 1912).
LEAF, W. *Homer and History* (London, 1915).
MYRES, J. L. *Who were the Greeks?* (Berkeley, 1930).
*Cambridge Ancient History*, vol. ii (Cambridge, 1924).

# 5

## *The Near East in the Twelfth Century B.C.*

IN Chapter 3 we left Egypt in a state of anarchy. About 1200 B.C. there arose a strong man of uncertain origin, who re-established order; this was Setnakht, believed to have been a descendant of Seti I and Ramses II. He ascended the throne as first monarch of the 20th Dynasty, and had scarcely had time to do more than quell the insurrection, when he died in 1198 B.C., leaving his kingdom to his son, who succeeded as Ramses III.

Young and vigorous, the new king lost no time before re-organizing his army, and, since good fighting men were scarce in Egypt, he was forced to have recourse to mercenaries. He retained the services of the Sherden or Shardana, who came originally, it is believed, from Sardis, and added to these a contingent of Kehek from the Libyan desert. His reorganization was effected none too soon, for in 1194 B.C. his kingdom was attacked by a great host, coming mostly in wagons down the Syrian coast, and partly in ships from the same direction.

Let us give the account of the attack in the words of his scribes. 'The isles were restless, disturbed among themselves; they poured out their people all together. No land stood before them, beginning from the Khatti, Kode, Carchemish, Arvad, and Alasya; they destroyed them and assembled together in their camp in the midst of the Amorite country.' Later on the scribes continue: 'They marched towards Egypt with fire prepared before them. P-l-s-t, Z-kk-r, Sh-k-l-sh, D-n-y-n, and W-sh-sh were their strength. These lands were united; they laid their hands upon the countries as far as the circle of the world.' 'The countries which came from their isles in the midst of the sea, they advanced upon Egypt, their hearts relying upon their arms.'

The names of these people have been variously transliterated and identified. Ramses evidently believed that some of them came from the isles of the Aegean, and a few of the later commentators have adopted this view. Others, however, as we shall see, have identified most of them with people living in the south of Asia Minor.

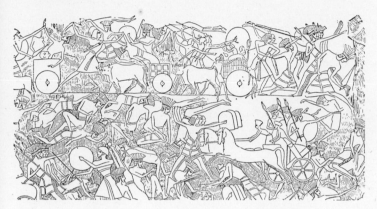

FIG. 19. Philistines defeated by Egyptians and Shardana.

The word P-l-s-t has been read Peleset and Pulisati, and these people have been identified with the Philistines. Burn points out that they had head-gear surrounded by feathers, and that this feather crown is worn by Ionian and Carian warriors in an Assyrian relief and by the Lycians in the army of Xerxes. This suggests that the P-l-s-t came from the south-west corner of Asia Minor, a view that had already been advanced by Hall. Myres has suggested that the words Pulisata, Palestine, and Philistine are connected with the words Pelasgian, Pelops, and Peloponnese. This may very likely be the case, since it was said that there had been Pelasgians in the neighbourhood of Cnidos before the foundation of that city, while Strabo says that the

Leleges and Pelasgi were driven out of Caria on the arrival of the Carians from Crete.

Z-kk-r has been written Thekel, Zakkal, Djakarat, and Zakkaru, though the last form is that now generally adopted. Myres compares the word with Zakro in Crete, and suggests that they were Teucrians. Hall denied the connexion with Teucrians, but accepted the identification with Zakro, while Burn, with more probability, believes them to have come from Zikhria, a place added to the Hittite empire by Murshil. The Sh-k-l-sh, variously written as Shakalsha, Shekelesh, and Shekhlal, seem to have been men from Sagalassos in the north of Pisidia.

The D-n-y-n are usually written Danuna, Daanan, and Danana, and are almost unanimously identified with the Danaans; in fact Childe considers their identity certain. It may be questioned, however, whether the Danaans, who were the inhabitants of Argolis and the subjects of Agamemnon, could have undertaken such an expedition in 1194 B.C., if, as we believe, that was the very year in which they started their attack on Troy. We would venture to suggest that they were, perhaps, the people of Tyana, later the capital of Cappadocia, and which seems to be the same as the Dana mentioned by Xenophon.

Finally the W-sh-sh, transliterated Washasha, Weshesh, Uashasha, and Uasha-sha, have been identified as the people of Oaxos in Crete by Hall and Myres, as the people of Issus on the Syrian coast by Sayce, and as the men of Oassos in Caria by Maspero, with whom Burn is in agreement. We are inclined to adopt the last of these suggestions.

If the views that we have advanced are correct, all these people came from the southern part of Asia Minor, and, as most of them advanced in wagons, we may be sure that they were fleeing with their families and property from some disturbing element at home. We have already noted that about 1200 B.C.

the Hittite documents come to an abrupt end, and we can hardly doubt that these people were leaving their homes owing to the downfall of the paramount power.

This is our opportunity for discussing the downfall of the Hittite empire. We have seen in Chapter 3 that soon after 1300 B.C., probably about 1270 B.C., the Phrygians crossed the Hellespont and took possession of the north-west corner of Asia Minor. A generation later, when Priam was a young man, they advanced south-westward as far as the river Sangarius, where they were attacked by the Amazons, who were repulsed with difficulty. It seems likely, however, that about the year 1200 B.C. they again pushed eastwards, this time with success, and brought to an end the Hittite empire in Asia Minor, when many of its subject peoples fled with their families down the Syrian coast. Whether it was with a view to assisting the Hittites that the Achaean force set out for Troy, or whether it was a desire to share the spoil, or merely to free the straits from oppressive dues while its possessors were scarce recovered from their exertions, it is difficult to determine. Perhaps all these motives entered into the calculations of Agamemnon.

The horde of refugees, travelling with their families in heavy, two-wheeled ox-carts, was sufficiently numerous and powerful to overcome the resistance of the peoples of the Syrian coast. They occupied all north Syria as far as Carchemish on the Euphrates, and devastated the kingdom of Amor in the Orontes valley; the advance guard forced their way to the frontiers of Egypt. Ramses assembled his army and fleet and took command; he drove back those that had reached his frontiers, then met and defeated the main body on the borders of Amor. The W-sh-sh, who seem to have been in the van, were captured and retained as slaves in Egypt. The Sh-k-l-sh, who were with them, made peace with the king and were retained as mercenaries. The P-l-s-t, who had followed these, were defeated just north of the frontier, and having capitulated were allowed to occupy the coastal plain beneath the Judaean plateau, where they remained as Philistines until defeated by David shortly after 1000 B.C. Their name survives in that of Palestine.

The Z-kk-r settled near them on the Palestine coast, north of Der near Mount Carmel, while it seems likely that the D-n-y-n, who were bringing up the rear, settled in north Syria and left their name in that of the town of Dana, east of Antioch. When these people had departed from the south of Asia Minor, the Cilices moved from the region just south of the Troad and settled in the district thereafter known as Cilicia.

After this campaign Ramses was not allowed to rest in peace, for soon afterwards he had to defend his country against the Meshwesh, who dwelt in the desert beyond the Libyans, and who were anxious to settle in the Delta. Lastly he had again to go to Syria, for many of its cities had revolted, and the remnant of the Hittites, expelled from Asia Minor, were endeavouring to create a small domain in what had formerly been one of their outlying provinces. Ramses was on the whole successful, and proceeded to organize his Asiatic possessions.

For a time Egypt was at peace and trade began again to expand in the Levant and in the Red Sea. The country became richer and the king bestowed extensive gifts upon the temples of the gods, and especially on those of Amon. This custom of endowing the temples was of long standing in Egypt, and since, although laymen might come and go, priesthoods remained for ever, a very large share of the wealth of the nation had come into priestly hands. The Harris papyrus, dating from this time, gives us a detailed account of the extent of this ecclesiastical property, and this shows us that the temples between them held 107,000 slaves, or 2 per cent. of the population, nearly 750,000 acres of land, more than $14\frac{1}{2}$ per cent. of the cultivable land in the country, about 500,000 head of cattle, 88 vessels, 53 workshops and shipyards, and 169 towns in Egypt and its dependencies. Such was the total property divided among the temples of all the gods but Knum, whose estates are omitted from the inventory; by far the greater part of this was in the hands of the priesthood of Amon.

So much of the wealth of the country had passed under the control of the priesthood, owing to the lavish gifts of his predecessors, that the treasury of Ramses was frequently empty, and the free peasants on the verge of starvation. The army no longer consisted of free men, for the king was unable to pay them; in their place he employed a number of foreign slaves from Syria, Asia Minor, and Libya. This was an unhealthy state of affairs, and dissatisfaction was felt throughout the whole kingdom. First his vizier rebelled and shut himself up in a city in the Delta. Then there was a palace plot. Tiy, one of the queens, endeavoured to secure the crown for her son, Pentewere, and during this revolt an attempt was made to assassinate the king. Though severely wounded Ramses survived and ordered a commission of fourteen judges to try the conspirators, who were found guilty and ordered to take their own lives. Soon after this Ramses III died in 1167 B.C., when the kingdom passed to his son Ramses IV.

We know little of the kingdom of Babylon at this time, except that it was still in the hands of the Kassites. Meli-shepak II was reigning in 1202 B.C., and a few years later attacked Ninurta-apel-ekur, who had become king of Assyria about the same time. This attack was unsuccessful, and we hear little more of Meli-shepak before his death in 1187 B.C., when he was succeeded by Marduk-apal-eddin I. Ninurta-apel-ekur died in 1175 B.C. and was succeeded on the throne of Assyria by Ashur-dam I, and in 1174 B.C. Ilbaba-shum-iddin became king of Babylon. In the same year Ashur-dam attacked Karduniash and captured the towns of Zaban, Irriya, and Akarsalla, but the following year the Elamites, under Shutrul-Nahkhunte, swept down from the mountains and slew Ilbaba-shum-iddin, who was succeeded at Babylon by Enlil-nadin-akhe, after whose death in 1169 B.C. the Kassite kingdom came to an end.

Troy, as we have endeavoured to show in Chapter 1, was

FIG. 20.   Map of the Near East.

sacked by the Achaeans in 1184 B.C., but the evidence from the excavations shows that the city was not destroyed until nearly a century later. If we may judge from a prophecy, put into the mouth of Poseidon yet written after the event, Aeneas gathered together the remnant of his people, after the expulsion of the house of Priam, and reigned there for a time, and was succeeded in turn by his son and grandson.

The Achaean heroes met misfortunes during or after their return from Troy. More than one fell on the battle-field, leaving their houses without heirs, thus completing that race suicide, to which, as Hesiod has pointed out, their many wars were tending. Menelaus and Odysseus lost their way and were carried far by contrary winds and currents before they reached their homes. Agamemnon regained his capital without adventure, but on his arrival found that his cousin Aegisthus had during his absence appropriated his kingdom and his wife; immediately on his return he fell a victim to the axe wielded by Clytemnestra. Orestes, his son, still a boy, fled for a time, but returned when grown up to avenge his father's death. A few years later he married his cousin Hermione, the daughter of Menelaus and Helen, and together they ruled the Peloponnese for some years. About 1190 B.C. the city of Tyre was rebuilt and reorganized, and became the most important port on the Syrian coast, later eclipsing the older city of Sidon. About 1176 B.C., probably on the return of Orestes to the Peloponnese, some of the Achaeans migrated to Cyprus, where they introduced the Arcadian dialect.

We must now return to Egypt, where Ramses IV ascended the throne in 1167 B.C. He gave his father a magnificent funeral, and had compiled a full list of his benefactions to the temples, which has come down to us as the Harris papyrus. He was completely under the domination of the priests, chief among which were the High Priest at el-Kab and the High Priest of Amon at Thebes. These officials really ruled the kingdom during his reign and that of his son Ramses V, who succeeded him in 1161 B.C., nor were his successors, Ramses VI, VII, and VIII, who ruled successively between 1157 and 1142 B.C., any more effective as kings. The power was gradually passing into the hands of Amenhotep, who had succeeded his father Ramsesnakht as High Priest of Amon at Thebes.

The Kassite rule at Babylon came to a close with the death of Enlil-nadin-akhe in 1169 B.C. Of his end we know nothing, but that at his death the rule at Babylon came into the hands of the Pashe, who seem to have been rulers of Isin. The only king of this line, usually spoken of as the 2nd Dynasty of Isin, who was of any consequence, was Nebuchadrezzar I, who succeeded to the throne in 1147 B.C.

Ashur-dam I was ruling Assyria, and seems to have been making that kingdom the most influential in the Near East. Only once was his power seriously threatened. This was some time between 1170 and 1160 B.C., when the Muski raided his territory. These Muski or Mazki, afterwards called Moschoi by the Greeks and Mesech by the Hebrews, seem to have been one of the Phrygian tribes, who had been in the vanguard during the attack on the Hittite empire in Asia Minor. They appear to have settled in what was afterwards Cappadocia, and fixed their capital at Tyana, though, if they can be identified with the Mazaka, they were living at an earlier date near Mount Argeus, some thirty miles to the north-west. These people seem to have been attempting to annex the territory in Syria still in Hittite hands, and advanced towards the Euphrates and crossed it into the provinces of Alzi or Alshe and Purukuzzi. Here they were allowed to settle for a time, though the king of Babylon took steps to prevent them from encroaching on his boundary.

During this time the Hebrew tribes, settled in the uplands of Palestine, were from time to time coalescing for defence against their enemies under the leadership of magistrates, known as Judges. The one unifying element centred round the ark and the common worship at Shiloh, where Eli was High Priest about the middle of the 12th century, when Edom became a kingdom. At the same time also Orestes was succeeded as ruler of the Peloponnese by his son Tisamenos.

In 1142 B.C., as we have seen, Ramses IX ascended the throne of Egypt, and ten years later we find him making still more valuable gifts to the High Priest of Amon at Thebes. These gifts further impoverished his already depleted treasury, and the poverty of his free subjects grew more acute. By 1126 B.C. this had become so severe that the people took to robbing the tombs in the Theban necropolis, until the king had to put a stop to such crimes with a severe hand. Meanwhile the influence of Egypt in foreign lands was waning, and we have clear evidence of this in an account that has come down to us of an Egyptian envoy, who

FIG. 21. Ramses IX decorating Amenhotep, High Priest of Amon.

was detained as a prisoner by the chief of Byblos. At last the king's rule became so weak that in 1123 B.C. he associated with him on the throne a son, who is known as Ramses X, and five years later, in 1118 B.C., he died, when he was succeeded by Ramses XI.

This king was no more an effective ruler than his predecessors and was equally under the control of the High Priest of Amon. As his rule weakened still further, his subjects became more and more dissatisfied, and in 1114 B.C. Nesubenebded, a noble of Tanis, rose in revolt and declared himself an independent king in the Delta. It was shortly after this that Hrihor, the High Priest of Amon, wished to send an envoy to the Lebanon to secure timber for building the sacred barque of Amon. That this journey might be made, permission had to be obtained from Nesubenebded to enable the envoy, Wen-amon, to pass through the Delta, and when he stopped for a time at Dor, he was robbed of the little money that he possessed, and was unable to obtain satisfaction from the Zakkaru prince of that city. After waiting nine days he proceeded by way of Tyre to Byblos, where he was refused admission by Zakar-baal, the lord of the city, and was told to leave without delay. At length, after many further adventures, he reached home without having carried out his mission. After this Ramses became still more subservient to the High Priest, and at his death in 1100 B.C., Hrihor and Nesubenebded divided the kingdom between them, the latter considering himself as the first king of the 21st Dynasty.

In 1115 B.C. Tiglathpileser I became king of Assyria. Soon after he ascended the throne he drove the Muski out of the provinces of Alzi and Purukuzzi, where they had been settled for about fifty years. Five kings of this people had attacked Kummukh, or Commagene, but Tiglathpileser drove them out. He then proceeded to annex the district thus relieved from the Muski, but the Hittite ruler of this city, Kili-Teshub, refused to pay taxes to the Assyrian king. He was therefore removed and the whole area attached to the Assyrian kingdom, after which Tiglathpileser absorbed also all the other Hittite territories in the neighbourhood. In 1107 B.C. Marduk-nadin-akhe, king of Babylon, made a raid into Assyria, but was promptly checked by Tiglathpileser, who captured many cities in Babylonia. The king of Assyria was now the most powerful monarch in the Near East. Even the last remnant of the Hittite empire had disappeared in 1115 B.C., Babylonia was becoming weaker, and none of the petty states on the Syrian coast of the Mediterranean had much influence. Through the latter territories Tiglathpileser

Fig. 22. Divine emblems on a charter of Nebuchadrezzar I.

led his army in 1100 B.C., and arrived on the frontier of Egypt. Nesubenebded, the king of the Delta, was much alarmed at his approach and hastened to send envoys to the frontier to conciliate him. These brought with them a crocodile as a present to the Assyrian king, who seems to have been satisfied with his reception, and Egypt was thus saved from an armed invasion.

About 1130 B.C., or perhaps some years later, the Dorians, who had been wandering along the foot-hills of Pindus in the west of Thessaly, moved south and occupied the district of Doris on the northern slopes of Parnassus, and a little later, if we may believe Herodotus, some Tyrsenians left Lydia, because of a famine, and sailed for Italy, where they were afterwards known as Etruscans.

Tisamenos ruled the Peloponnese, apparently unmolested, for many years, but when he had grown to be an old man, his kingdom was overwhelmed. It was about 1104 B.C., according to tradition, that the Dorians crossed the Gulf of Corinth and entered the Peloponnese, and almost immediately the kingdom of Tisamenos, the last remnant of the former Achaean greatness, fell before the conquering heroes, whose movements we must leave to the next chapter.

About the same time, or perhaps a little earlier, the sixth settlement on the mound of Hissarlik, where Aeneas and his descendants had been ruling since the Trojan War, was attacked and demolished, and the Seventh City arose in its place. From the discovery here of fragments of pottery, decorated with concentric rings of impressed ornament, it is concluded that this attack had been made by people from central Europe, whose culture, known as that of Lausitz, will be more fully described later in this volume.

We cannot close this chapter without a word on what are known as the *thalassocracies*. Eusebius in his history quotes from Diodorus Siculus a list of those who ruled the sea from the fall of Troy to the Persian Wars. The books of Diodorus, in which these lists occur, are unfortunately lost, and it has been conjectured that he obtained his information from Castor of Rhodes, who is known to have written on the subject. This list of those ruling the Aegean, or *thalassocrats*, has been discussed by a number of writers, and Burn has recently suggested that

they date, not from the fall of Troy, which Eusebius places in
1172 B.C., but from the fall of Knossos, in or about 1400 B.C.
Here we give the list of sea-powers with both sets of dates.

|  |  | *Years.* | *Eusebius* 1172. | *Burn* 1400. |
|---|---|---|---|---|
| Lydians or Maeonians . | . | 92 | | |
| | | | 1080 | 1308 |
| Pelasgians . . . | . | 85 | | |
| | | | 995 | 1223 |
| Thracians . . . | . | 79 | | |
| | | | 916 | 1144 |
| Phrygians . . . | . | 25 | | |
| | | | 891 | 1119 |
| Rhodians . . . | . | 23 | | |
| | | | 868 | 1096 |
| Cypriotes . . . | . | 33 | | |
| | | | 835 | 1065 |
| Phoenicians . . | . | 45 | | |
| | | | 790 | 1020 |

BOOKS

BREASTED, J. H.  *A History of Egypt* (New York, 1912).
BURN, A. R.  *Minoans, Philistines, and Greeks* (London, 1930).
*Cambridge Ancient History*, vol. ii (Cambridge, 1924).
MYRES, J. L.  *Who were the Greeks?* (Berkeley, 1930).
ROBINSON, T. H.  *A History of Israel* (Oxford, 1932).

# 6

## *The Near East in the Eleventh Century* B.C.

WE have pointed out in Chapter 1 that after the fall of Knossos,
about 1400 B.C., a dark period followed in the Near East; this is
particularly true for Greek lands.  In our survey of the interval
between that event and the siege of Troy we were able to fall
back upon the testimony of tradition, and we attempted to trace
the course of the intervening history by relating the stories that
have come down to us from the Heroic Age.  After the sack of
Troy this type of evidence almost fails us.  We have, it is true,

a few stories dealing with the return of the heroes after the war and the misfortunes that befell them, but the only event of outstanding importance preserved by the folk memory of the Greeks was the coming of the Dorians. This, according to the traditions that we have followed in the previous chapter, took place in 1104 B.C. There are some reasons, however, to suspect, from the evidence supplied by recent excavations, that, while the tradition is substantially correct, the date of the event was about half a century later than was subsequently believed.

In Chapter 2 we suggested that the available evidence was best interpreted by stating that a group of Hellenes, afterwards known as the Dorians, left the south-west of the Maliac Gulf about 1400 B.C. and moved northwards into south-west Thessaly, whence they were driven a little later by the Cadmeians as far as the foot-hills of Ossa and Olympus. Soon after 1350 B.C. the Dorians were again driven out by the Cadmeians, and wandered westwards to the foot-hills of the Pindus range, to a place called Macednon, in which, perhaps, we may see an earlier form of the name Macedon. It is in this region that we first pick up some archaeological evidence.

At three sites in Macedonia, Buboshta, and Vardaroftsa in the south, and Chauchitza farther to the north-east, have been found the remains of late Bronze Age villages, the two first of which are believed by some to be those of the Dorians during the period when they dwelt in the region that Herodotus calls Macednon. On these sites the pottery closely resembles that introduced many centuries earlier into the Spercheios valley by the people that we believe to have been the first true Hellenes to settle in Hellas. This pottery seems to be ancestral to the wares that we meet with all over Greece at a slightly later date, wares which are known as geometric. At Buboshta there occurs, too, the meander pattern, a prominent element in the later geometric decoration as it was in the ornament of the earlier Dhimini ware.

This suggests that these villages were settlements of the Dorians, who had wandered up from near the mouth of the Spercheios,

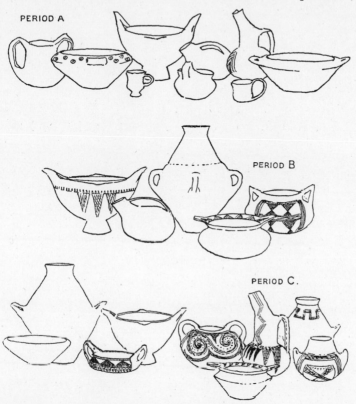

FIG. 23. Pottery from Vardaroftsa.

and had passed on their way by the region in which the Dhimini ware had been prevalent. Whether they carried with them the custom of painting their pottery with geometric patterns, a custom that had been abandoned in their old home on the introduction of the grey Minyan ware, is uncertain; they may have found it in use on their arrival in southern Macedon, since such pottery has been found all along the foot-hills of the Pindus range, from the Macedonian border to the Spercheios valley. We seem, however, to be on sound ground in accepting these

Fig. 24.  Lausitz pottery from Hissarlik VII.

settlements at Buboshta and Vardaroftsa, or the later stages of them at any rate, as being some of the abodes of the Dorians at this time.

The excavations have shown that Vardaroftsa, and Chauchitza as well, were destroyed by an iron-using people at a date that cannot be much earlier than 1100 B.C. That the destroyers were the people of the Lausitz culture, who reached Macedonia early in this century and went on to the founding of the seventh settlement at Hissarlik, we have already noted in Chapter 5. It seems probable that this invasion it was that caused the Dorians to move southwards through eastern Thessaly to the area later known as Doris, and ultimately to the Peloponnese.

The intrusion of the Lausitz people into Macedon seems to have led to other movements than those of the Dorians. It is perhaps to this time that we may attribute the departure of the Boeotians from the neighbourhood of Arne in the fertile plain of Aeolis to enter the land to which they gave their name. Some, however, believe that this movement took place a century earlier, when the Cadmeians had been expelled from Thebes, since Homer includes Boeotian contingents among the Achaean forces that set out for Troy. Folk tradition, on the other hand, was convinced that the Boeotians had been expelled from the Aeolian plain by an invasion of Thessalians, a body of wild mountaineers from Thesprotia, the district around Dodona, led by Achaean nobles who claimed descent from Heracles. These movements the ancient chronologists placed at 1184 B.C., just about the time of the Lausitz invasion of Macedon, while the Dorian invasion of the Peloponnese is placed twenty years later.

Though tradition and the works of the chronologists hang well together, these dates do not agree with the results of recent archaeological research. In Thessaly excavations have been carried out at several sites, on which there are clear signs of abrupt termination at a date which appears on archaeological grounds to be about 1050 B.C. About the same time, it would appear from similar evidence, the port of Korakou, near Corinth, was destroyed, Mycenae was burnt, and the town of Tiryns laid low and converted into a cemetery.

It is difficult to unite all these conflicting views, but the most likely reconstruction appears to us to be the following. About 1180 B.C., or perhaps a little earlier, the Lausitz people entered Macedon and laid waste that region, thereby displacing the Dorian tribes, who moved southwards, possibly into the plain of Thessaly, whence they drove the Boeotians into what was now to become Boeotia, whither some had perhaps moved a century earlier. Shortly afterwards the Dorians moved south again, this time into Doris, perhaps driven from the Aeolian plain by the Thessalians, who had crossed the mountains from Thesprotia. The arrival of the Dorians in Doris has been dated about 1130 B.C.

It was probably about fifty years later that the Dorians, having outgrown this very circumscribed territory, started again to wander. Some crossed the pass above Pindus and moved down the Daphnus valley to Naupactus, whence a short voyage took them across the narrow entrance of the Gulf of Corinth. Others passed south to Crissa and sailed thence to the northern shores of the Peloponnese, while the larger part moved south-eastwards, past Chaeronea and Thebes on their way to Attica. Having reached the outskirts of Athens they paused, for it had been said by an oracle that in their contest with the Athenians a king would be slain, and that victory would go to the people who had lost their monarch. They gave instructions to their men on no account to kill Codrus, the Athenian king, but he, knowing of the oracle, visited the Dorian camp in the night, picked a quarrel with the soldiers and fell in the brawl. When the Dorian leaders heard of this they left Athens undisturbed and passed on to Megara. Then they crossed the Isthmus, sacked the port at Korakou, and crossing the pass destroyed Mycenae and Tiryns and settled at Argos.

Let us now turn to Egypt, which we left divided between Nesubenebded, prince of Tanis in the Delta, and Hrihor, high priest of Amon in Thebes. Early in this century Hrihor, who seems to have had royal blood in his veins, resigned his pretensions to the throne, and his rival declared himself the first king of the 21st Dynasty. Nesubenebded had married a daughter of the last king of the previous dynasty, by whom he had a son, Psibkhenno, and a daughter, Henttoui, who married Piankh, son and successor of Hrihor. Nesubenebded restored several of the buildings of Thutmose III at Karnak, and died in 1070 B.C., when he was succeeded by Painozem, who was the son of Piankh, and like him high priest of Amon, and who had married Makere-Mutemhat, the sister of Psibkhenno. Painozem had three sons, Zedkhonsefankh, Masaherti, and Menkheperre, each of whom in turn became high priest of Amon; he ruled until his death in 1030 B.C., but little is known of the events of his reign.

Tiglathpileser I, king of Assyria, died in 1102 B.C., when he was succeeded by Ninurta-apal-ekut II, who was probably his son. He reigned until 1092 B.C., when he was followed by Ashurbal-kala, who was certainly a son of Tiglathpileser. The following year the Assyrian king entered into friendly relations with Marduk-shapik-zer-mati, who had succeeded Marduk-balatu-akhe, king of Isin. In 1083 B.C. Adad-apal-iddin succeeded to the kingdom of Isin, and in 1075 B.C. Ashurbal-kala was driven from the throne of Assyria by Enlil-rabi, and took refuge at Sippar, though he recovered his kingdom in 1069 B.C. There seems to have been further trouble about 1060 B.C., when Eriba-Adad appears as king, and about 1050 B.C. Ashurbal-kala was succeeded by his brother Shamshi-Adad IV. Meanwhile Marduk-akhe-eriba became king of Isin in 1061 B.C. and Marduk-zer- . . . in 1060 B.C.

We know little or nothing about what happened in Greece after the Dorians had destroyed what remained of the Achaean power. Tradition is almost silent. Herodotus tells us that they were first called Dorians when they entered the Peloponnese; this seems unlikely, since their name was preserved in the little state of Doris from which they had come. The genealogies of their two lines of kings have been handed down, but authorities differ as to their value.

There is a complete break in the archaeological record, for the old Achaean cities were destroyed and deserted, and we are uncertain how far back we can take the later settlements. It seems to be agreed that the Dorians had learnt the use of iron weapons, probably from the Lausitz people, who had dislodged them from their Macedonian home, and who had brought with them iron swords from Hungary. It was the possession of these new and superior arms that enabled them to gain such an easy victory over their Achaean opponents.

As long as the Achaean rule survived, the pottery in use was a late type of the Mycenean ware, originally introduced from Crete. This is found on all sites up to 1050 B.C. of such a uniform kind that we must suppose that these wares were made by mass production at a few sites, and thence exported over the whole of the Achaean world as far north as Macedon. With the great destruction that occurred about 1050 B.C. this Mycenean ware entirely disappeared and we must conclude that the centres of its manufacture were destroyed and the potters dispersed or killed. In all later settlements we find much rougher pottery, of a totally different type, always decorated with geometric ornament, but in various styles in each locality; this suggests that the potter's art had ceased to be an organized trade and had reverted to its original position as the women's industry.

It is natural to suppose that this new ware, found so generally throughout Greek lands, was introduced by the invading Dorians. Against this, however, several arguments may be urged. We have no evidence that the Dorians used this kind of ware before they started on their wanderings; it is difficult to date any known pieces before 1000 B.C., while the most typical forms of this ware were made at Athens, just outside the Dipylon gate, and, as we have seen, Athens was the one city in Greece unaffected by the Dorian conquest.

In some ways the geometric wares remind us of the pottery introduced many centuries earlier into the Spercheios valley, and we have seen that such wares survived nearly up to this time on the slopes of Mount Pindus; they may well have survived in remote villages elsewhere, and laid the foundation for the various geometric wares that arose at this time all over the land.  The decoration of some of the early geometric pots suggests that they were made in imitation of rush baskets, and it may be that all or

Fig. 25.  Various types of geometric pottery.

most of them arose from copying in pottery the basket wares used by the village women.  By the middle of the tenth century such wares came into general use throughout Greek lands, but there was never any uniformity of style, each region decorating its pots in its own way.

The Dorian invasion not only brought to an end the Achaean

power, it ended also the trading activities carried on by the Myceneans or Cretans settled on the mainland. These, who had long adopted Hellenic speech, were known, it would appear, as Ionians, and they were not content to remain under the barbaric rule of their Dorian conquerors. The same was true of other subjects of the Achaean monarchy. In 1053 B.C. some Aeolians settled in Lesbos, and this gives us a possible date for the first movement of the Dorians from Doris. In 1044 B.C., according to tradition, occurred the great Ionic migration, when the majority of the traders in the Peloponnese sailed across the Aegean to settle on the coast of Asia Minor. About the same time such Achaeans as were left settled on the southern shore of the Gulf of Corinth. Thus began that great movement, the foundation of the Greek colonies, which will occupy our attention in our next volume. Here we need only mention the foundation of Cyme in 1033 B.C. and of Smyrna in 1015 B.C.

Meanwhile the Phoenicians, the people of Tyre and Sidon, who had profited by the fate of Knossos, still further increased their overseas trade when the cities of Greece ceased to export their wares. They traded at first with the east through the Red Sea, and then pushed farther and farther to the west, though their chief colonies in this direction were not founded until a later date.

The whole of Greece with the exception of Athens, was now under Dorian rule and rapidly relapsed into barbarism; neither tradition nor archaeology gives us even a glimpse of what was taking place. The Dorians seem to have been essentially hill-folk, and to have preferred the more mountainous parts of the land, but, as far as we can judge from the results of excavations, they did not found the city of Sparta, afterwards their capital, until about 950 B.C.

At his death in 1030 B.C. Painozem in Egypt was succeeded by his third son, Menkhepere, who had already become high priest of Amon, but his accession was disputed by Amenophet, prince of Tanis, who succeeded him about 1020 B.C. Menkhepere retained the position of high priest until his death about 1010 B.C., when it devolved upon his elder son, Nesubenebded, who held it for but a short time, after which he was succeeded by his brother Painozem II, who was high priest until the time of his death about 954 B.C. Amenophet died in 970 B.C., when he was succeeded by Siamon, who died in 950 B.C.; then followed Hor-Psibkhenno, who was driven from the throne in 942 B.C. by Shishak, the founder of the 22nd Dynasty.

During this century the Philistines were dominating the whole of Palestine, though about 1025 B.C. the Hebrews made gallant attempts under Saul to free their country from this foreign yoke. This was eventually effected by David, who seems to have succeeded his predecessor about 1015 B.C. About 1000 B.C. the power of the Philistines was broken, and the Hebrew state enjoyed a period of prosperity under David and his son Solomon, until the death of the latter about 933 B.C.

Nabu-shum-libur became king of Isin in 1047 B.C. and reigned until 1039 B.C., when his line came suddenly to an end. The previous year the Hatti or Hittites from north Syria had attacked the southern part of Mesopotamia, and this may account for the sudden collapse of the dynasty. Ever since the time of Tiglathpileser I certain desert tribes from the borders of north Syria had been threatening the Assyrian frontier. These, known as Aramaeans, were kept off by Tiglathpileser, though after his death many of them settled within the Assyrian border. Later on they, and with them the Kaldu or Chaldaeans, invaded southern Mesopotamia, and it was probably their appearance near the head of the Persian Gulf that brought the kingdom of Isin to an end.

Shamshi-Adad IV was succeeded in 1038 B.C. on the throne of Assyria by Ashur-nasir-pal, his son, who was in turn succeeded

by Shulmanu-asharid, commonly called Shalmaneser II, about
1020 B.C.  Shalmaneser was followed in 1008 B.C. by Ashur-
nirari IV, who reigned until 1002 B.C., when Ashur-rabi II
founded a new dynasty.

### BOOKS

BREASTED, J. H.  *A History of Egypt* (New York, 1912).
BURN, A. R.  *Minoans, Philistines, and Greeks* (London, 1930).
*Cambridge Ancient History*, vol. iii (Cambridge, 1925).
MYRES, J. L.  *Who were the Greeks?* (Berkeley, 1930).
ROBINSON, T. H.  *A History of Israel* (Oxford, 1932).

# 7

## *East-Central Europe*

IN the Early Bronze Age metallurgy was developed at but few
centres, and articles were traded as finished products and were
accordingly rare.  Later, we have more definite evidence of a
route of trade from the Baltic coast to the Hungarian plain, up
the Elbe and through Bohemia, or through the Franconian Jura.
This route led to the head of the Adriatic Sea and developed a
branch through the Inn valley and the Brenner pass.  Though
this is often called the amber-route, implements of bronze and
the tin of Bohemia were important items in its trade.  The
spread of the latter helped to increase the number of centres of
bronze craftsmanship.

Villages meanwhile multiplied on the loess areas; the inhabitants of these grew grain and kept horses, cattle, and
especially pigs.  Domestic animals were increasingly used in
agricultural work, population increased and villages and their
field systems became more durable.  The villagers' needs expanded, and this period gives many hoards of bronze implements, whole or broken, that must have been the property of
travelling tinkers, going from village to village as in later times.

In spite of the increase of permanent villages there is no evidence from this period of the rise of anything like a city in central Europe; that stage of development was still far in the future. None the less the conditions now known to have

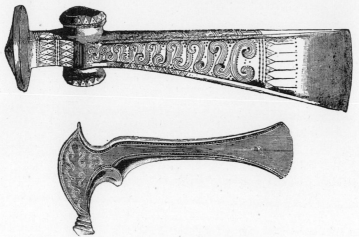

Fig. 26. Bronze battle-axes from Hungary.

obtained in central Europe in the Bronze Age make it interesting that, even at the end of the nineteenth century, it was possible to question whether settled agricultural life existed east of the Rhine before Roman times.

Travelling tinkers and trade-routes helped to spread fashions in particular objects, and a locality with a special heritage of civilization could henceforth acquire some new fashion in its industries, or some new type of article, to add to its own equipment. In other words, a form of culture could now become altered by the addition of an extraneous idea without serious revolution. It follows that the power of sheer tradition was weakening, and that initiative was gaining in vigour; this is an important prelude to the immense developments of abstract ideas that become so potent in the last millennium B.C.

Already for the late Bronze Age the students' task is made harder by the complications just mentioned; he may give a high and far-off date to one find and a later date to another, though perhaps they were contemporary, just because the first did not, while the second did, include some new-fashioned object, brought probably by a travelling tinker.

From the steppe of south Russia in this dry warm period the horsemen had moved away, some in the direction of the copper-yielding Slovakian hills to the north of Hungary. Their characteristic weapon was the battle-axe or hammer of metal, with its shaft-tube lengthened both ways beyond the body of the axe; the butt end of the axe was variously developed and, in later forms, often associated in some way with the shaft-tube. Myres is undoubtedly right in thinking that these battle-axes were wielded by horsemen, and bridle-bits have been found.

The people from the Lausitz area, lying on the loess between the Elbe and the Oder, seem to have been physically, as well as culturally, in a large measure the successors of the people with the Aunjetitz culture in the same region. Their villages contained a number of wooden houses, set close together, each house having a porch and main-room, a plan resembling that of the *megaron* of the north Aegean region. The villages developed strong defences as time went on.

In this culture of the Lausitz area cremation of the dead replaced burial. The body was burned at a special place, and the remains were collected, cleaned from wood-ash, and placed in an urn which was pitcher-shaped and covered by a dish. The urns were buried, often without any protection, in an urn-field, though occasionally a mound was raised. In some of the earlier urns there is a hole, either broken through the pot or specially bored; this is often called by German students the *Seelenloch*, from the fancy that it was intended as an opening for the egress of the soul.

The early pitcher of the Lausitz area had an inverted cone at its base. The bulbous portion above this was sharply separated from a short wide neck, and the junction between the bulbous

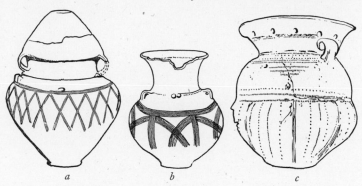

*a*        *b*        *c*

FIG. 27. The Urn-field culture and its pottery. *a, b* from Lovasberény; *c* from Temes-Kubin.

portion and the neck was marked by one, two, or four handles. The bulbous part was usually adorned with large *mammae*, which in process of time were diminished to small warts, sometimes in the centre of a series of concentric circles; often there were flutings as well on the bulbous surface.

Childe has distinguished several cultures of the Middle and Late Bronze Ages in west and south Hungary. Here and there we find corded lines of ornament on the pots, probably an indication of influences from the Russian steppe border, the early pottery of which is discussed in Chapter 3 of *The Way of the Sea*. In south Hungary also are found female figurines, which seem to show Aegean affinities. The Lausitz culture early influenced the west and south of Hungary, but eventually it also penetrated into, and triumphed among, the people of the Slovakian region. In the south-west the pots of these cultures are often copied from metal models, and include some extremely fine ware known as Pannonian. The custom of burying the cremated dead in an urn-field spread widely.

The west, centre, and south of Hungary at this time, as befitted the region of non-Mediterranean Europe with the

FIG. 28. Examples of Pannonian ware.

longest tradition of civilization, had become a focus of fashions and a melting-pot of cultures. It was during the Bronze Age, also, that the better wheats, known to botanists as the 42-chromosome wheats, varieties of *Triticum vulgare* or the bread wheat, displaced in central Europe in a general way the older wheats such as small spelt, *Triticum monococcum*, a 14-chromo-some variety.

In earlier phases the civilization of the Middle Danube had a cousinly relation with the Aunjetitz culture, and was deeply indebted to stimuli from the Aegean; now at the close of the Middle Bronze Age there were trends of influence for a time in both directions. From the Aegean still came, as of old, fashions in figurines and many other things; to the Aegean probably went, as we shall see, the idea of the sword. The people of the steppe borders, judging from Rumania, seem to have been rather poor in the Bronze Age, apart from a few results of the exploitation of the copper of Baia de arama, north-west of the Iron Gates; this is natural if the steppe was suffering from drought. While, in the full Bronze Age, culture in the Balkan peninsula was related to that of Hissarlik and Asia Minor, towards the end of that period men of the steppe border advanced through that region, as we have seen in previous chapters. The tin of Bohemia and the gold and copper of the Slovakian mountains, east and west Transylvania, and the eastern Alps must have been of great importance.

Though stone tools remained in use, bronze axes, of the type known as palstaves, had spread into the Danubian region, apparently through Bohemia. Pins and long spiral coils of wire serving as arm-rings were much in vogue, and ornaments of bronze and gold became numerous. Some pendants suggest links with the Aegean.

Two matters relating to east-central Europe and its connexions with the Aegean are of special importance. They are the spread of the sword and of the *fibula* or safety-pin.

The simple copper or bronze dagger, with a hilt riveted on to the blade, is common in the Early Bronze Age, and is of very widespread occurrence, though distinctly a feature of the Beaker people in central Europe. At the dawn of its Metal Age the flint dagger is characteristic of the west Baltic region. Some German students, deeply impressed by the fine workmanship on these weapons from the west Baltic, have suggested that from that region the world received both the battle-axe and the sword. We have already in various places in the *Corridors of Time* argued for the view of Sophus Müller, who considered these objects introductions into the Baltic from the south-east.

In the Aegean region the copper dagger, in use at the beginning of the second millennium B.C., gave birth to a longer weapon, the dirk, often called a rapier; and dirks, showing influences from the Aegean, spread throughout central Europe. The dirk was of obvious value to the pedestrian, but on horseback a slashing weapon would be more useful, and we think that it was somewhere among the horse-riding men of the later Bronze Age that the dirk gave birth to the sword. Probably also, as Childe suggests, a swifter horse had by this time spread in from the steppes.

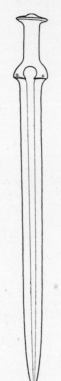

FIG. 29. Sword with full metal hilt, derived from dagger.

A dirk is a thrusting weapon, and most specimens have blades less than 2 feet in length. The sword blade is usually more than 2 feet long and may reach 3 feet; it is a slashing as well as a thrusting weapon. Often the two cutting edges are parallel one with the other until they approach the point, but many have a broadening of the blade either near the butt or half-way along; these weapons, which must have been used as hatchets as well as for slashing, are called leaf-shaped swords. Daggers, dirks, and swords have two main types of grip or hilt. In some this is cast in metal complete, either with rivets fastening its expanded shoulders to the butt end of the blade, or cast in one piece with the blade. In others the base of the blade is prolonged into a tongue which is pierced by holes; this tongue was flanked by plates, of wood or some other material, on both sides, and these plates were fastened together by rivets working through the holes in the metal tongue. To keep the plates firmly in position, the riveting was supplemented by the development of flanges on the tongue, and this idea, at any rate, was born in the Aegean.

We think the lengthening of the dirk into the sword may have occurred at nearly the same time in Greece and in central Europe, where the Mycenean dirk was well known. In Hungary there are early swords both with cast-metal hilts and with tongue grips, and some of them have the shoulders standing out well. The type with the full metal hilt is so obviously derived from a dagger that no more concerning it need here be said.

Some of the early examples with a tongue-grip have a characteristic spiral ornament on the blade, and, while mainly Hungarian, they have also been noted in one case from north-east Italy, and in another from Schleswig Holstein. They have the blade expanded near the butt end. Other Hungarian bronze swords with tongue-grips have the shoulders at the junction of the grip and blade less prominent, and one of us has suggested, in *The Bronze Age and the Celtic World* (1922), that these may be later types. The wider shoulders are clearly an inheritance from the dagger, in which the grip was riveted on to the blade, and they have little meaning in the swords with tongue-grips; indeed they seem gradually to be transformed into, or replaced by, projections that act as hand-guards. From a comparison of types one would expect that the earlier swords would have semicircular butts (*a*),*

Fig. 30. Sword with spiral ornament on blade.

and that these would be followed by semi-oval butts (*b, c*), these again by straight sloping shoulders with rounded corners (*d*), and lastly by similar shoulders without the rounded corners (*e*).

* These letters refer to the types discussed in the book named above.

It seems, however, that the swords with semi-oval butts appeared almost as early as those in which the butt is semicircular, and these date, we believe, from the fifteenth century B.C. The semi-oval type, we think, came into more general use as time went on. Of the swords with straight shoulders, those with the corners rounded seem on the whole to be later than the others,

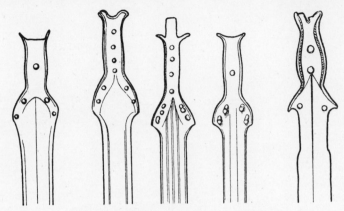

Fig. 31.   Tongue-grip swords from Hungary.

for, though the latter have been found in Hungary, they appear also in considerable numbers in the British Isles during the Late Bronze Age.   Childe gives one of the Danubian swords with straight shoulders a very early date, and we are prepared to agree with this view. We believe that they may first have appeared as early as the fourteenth century B.C., but that they lasted on in central Europe into the eleventh, while they were introduced into the British Isles at a still later date.   Swords of these types are known from Italy and the eastern Mediterranean.

A sword with full hilt in cast metal may belong to the period of the above-mentioned tongue-grip swords.   In it the hilt is a little expanded at the middle, and it is ribbed.   The pommel has a terminal knob. Later Hungarian swords with full metal hilts often have these parts highly decorated in a geometrical style, and the pommel in such swords does not develop long projections.

The *fibula* or safety-pin becomes in the course of evolution a most important index of cultural relations. A thorn, a pointed stick of wood, or a metal pin might have been used to fasten together two edges of textile material, but, to make the fastening effective, some further device was necessary. One of the earliest was that of winding a thread around the thorn or pin on both sides, and then an obvious improvement was effected by making a hole through which to pass the thread, or later the wire. An alternative scheme was reached by bending the pin and bringing the two bent ends into touch with one another. To strengthen the pin's grip the pin-head was complicated by the addition of a spiral curve that functioned as a spring. The pin-head was also hammered into a groove or catch to hold the point. The bow, or the half without the pin-point, was variously curved or bent to give space for holding more folds of cloth.

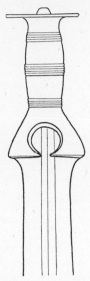

Fig. 32. Sword with full metal hilt, in cast metal.

It was formerly very generally thought that the *fibula* or safety-pin originated in the Middle Danube basin in the later part of the Bronze Age. Reinecke, Blinkenberg, and Myres think that it is, basically, an Aegean device which spread thence, especially during a period of expansion about the thirteenth century B.C. The mid-Danube region has yielded simple one-piece *fibulae*, as at Vinča, and also others in which the bow is prolonged beyond the catch into a spiral, sometimes larger than the rest of the brooch. These decorations, whether on the bow or beyond the catch, are, in Hungary, set in the plane that is common to bow and pin. This feature of the ornament 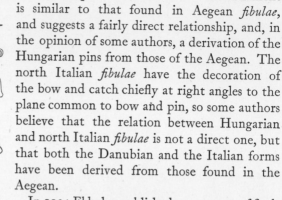 is similar to that found in Aegean *fibulae*, and suggests a fairly direct relationship, and, in the opinion of some authors, a derivation of the Hungarian pins from those of the Aegean. The north Italian *fibulae* have the decoration of the bow and catch chiefly at right angles to the plane common to bow and pin, so some authors believe that the relation between Hungarian and north Italian *fibulae* is not a direct one, but that both the Danubian and the Italian forms have been derived from those found in the Aegean.

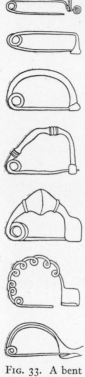

In 1924 Ekholm published an account of finds at Gemeinlebarn in Lower Austria from burials with objects indicating a station of Aunjetitz, that is fairly early Bronze Age, culture; some of the pins demonstrate this clearly. Yet this grave has yielded a *fibula* with four spirals at the bend between the bow and the pin. Ekholm argues thence that the origin of the *fibula* goes farther back in time than the views of Reinecke and others would lead one to suppose, and that its original home may well not have been the Aegean. Reinecke has wondered whether the *fibula* really belongs to the burial with which it was found; he speaks of cremation burials at Gemeinlebarn and thinks that the site was occupied for a long period; he believes, too, that the *fibula* in question is comparable with a type occurring during the transition from the Bronze to the Iron Age. If Ekholm's view is maintained, we may have to think that the origin of the *fibula*

FIG. 33. A bent pin and Fibulae.

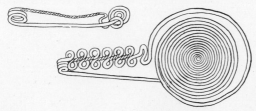

FIG. 34. Fibulae.

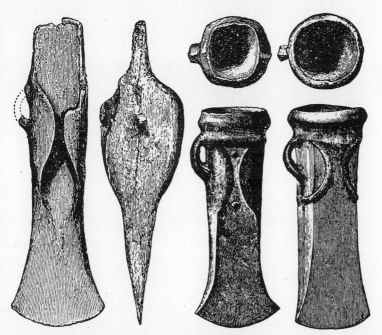

FIG. 35. A winged axe and a socketed axe with wings marked.

was in central Europe, though types which might be considered primitive are decidedly rare there. Childe thinks that at Gemeinlebarn a group of people with Aunjetitz culture may have persisted long after that culture had been superseded in most places, and that the group may have acquired objects of a later culture. Quite recently, however, *fibulae* have been found at other places in the Danube region in association with objects indicating an Aunjetitz culture, so there is an increasing probability that the *fibula* is older than has been supposed, while its place of origin must remain for the present an open question.

At some stage of the development of culture in the Lausitz area there appeared there a third remarkable item of the equipment of the Late Bronze Age, the socketed axe. It was formerly thought that the socketed axe had evolved from an axe with two wings near the base of its stem. The stem was fixed into split wood and the wings were bent round the wood to hold it in place. It was pointed out that some socketed axes had wings marked on them. This idea of axe-evolution has been given up.

The spear of bronze probably originated in a bronze ferrule binding the end of the wooden shaft. This is, in effect, a socket, and the socketed spear is undoubtedly far older than the socketed axe. It is possible that the idea of the socket was eventually transferred from one weapon to another, especially as this step meant economy in metal and obviated the previous danger of splitting the wooden shaft.

Another line of evolution is thought more probable still. In some bronze axes a tongue or tang was driven into a wooden handle and bronze rings were then fixed around that handle to prevent splitting. If these rings were cast in one piece with the axe itself, the result was a socket; the tang could be given up Some area of the Lausitz culture was the original home of the socketed axe; it was a superior weapon and had an important history, especially in western Europe.

Men gaining the use of horses, swords, socketed axes, *fibulae*, and the general metallurgical skill implied in the possession of these weapons and implements were obviously rising in the scale of civilization. It is highly significant of the dawn of a new phase of civilization that at least one, probably two and possibly three, of these novelties arose in Central Europe well away from the old *foci* of the eastern Mediterranean. Central Europe by this time had become a region of culture-mixture on a large scale.

Reference has already been made to the fact that the steppe-horsemen dominated the Slovakian region, doubtless also its copper and gold resources, which they defended by their traditional weapon, the battle-axe or hammer, the sacred emblem in Baltic mythology of the god Thor. In the course of time the rest of the mid-Danubian basin, receiving cultural contributions from north, and west, and south, had become richer in general equipment, and in all probability there was increased rivalry for control of the

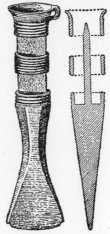

FIG. 36. A view of the origin of the socketed axe.

metalliferous areas. In the end the spear and sword, in the hands of the people who owed a great deal to the cultures of the Lausitz area, triumphed over the hammer or battle-axe. It was the passing of the supremacy from Thor to Odin. The Lausitz cultural influence spread southwards beyond the Danube basin to Macedonia and Asia Minor, as has been described in Chapters 4 and 6.

It is significant that swords of magic value play such a part in early legends. The power of swordsmen apparently made itself felt far and wide, and we seem there to touch the bases of legends of young heroes going to carve their fortunes, but of course this was a practice that long remained in vogue.

The leaders in this period apparently still had very long high heads and sharp profiles. These were described in Chapter 1 of *Merchant Venturers in Bronze* as one of the most characteristic types for the loess-areas of central Europe in the Early Bronze Age, and as related to earlier axe-hammer people of the steppe. This type, if we may judge by modern analogues, had a short upper lip, whereas the modern broad-headed peasantry of east-central Europe, probably already there in the Bronze Age, have the upper lip long. Of course, with the spread of cremation, the evidence about physical type becomes less, but there is every reason to think that at least these two types, and probably also a smaller long-headed type, including survivals of late Palaeolithic peoples, lived side by side, or perhaps in different social strata, in east-central Europe. The difference in the lips, just suggested, is of interest in connexion with language possibilities. The short upper lip makes the labial sounds difficult to pronounce clearly, while the long upper lip tends to make its possessors convert $k$ and $q$ sounds into $p$ sounds. If, as seems probable, Aryan speech was one of the possessions of the steppe-horsemen, the differentiation of languages emphasizing the $k$ or $q$ from those emphasizing the $p$ sound may be found, when more details of type have been discovered, to be connected with the learning, and adaptation, of Aryan languages by people differing in physical type from their early possessors. The standardization of languages emphasizing one or the other set of sounds may be related to the proportions of the two types and of their respective influences in the various populations either in the period here discussed or at some subsequent time.

## BOOKS

CHILDE, V. GORDON. *The Danube in Prehistory* (Oxford, 1929).
CHILDE, V. GORDON. *The Bronze Age* (Cambridge, 1930).
PEAKE, HAROLD. *The Bronze Age and the Celtic World* (London, 1922).

# 8
## Italy in the Late Bronze Age

IN studying the later part of the Bronze Age we are brought into touch with stages leading to a great change in the geographical setting of the streams of cultural influence. In the earlier volumes of this series it has been necessary to point repeatedly to the lands by the rivers of Mesopotamia, Syria, and Egypt as the sources of a number of movements of cultures which included among other arts that of tilling the land. From the fifth volume onwards the archaeological record shows that the agricultural and maritime life implanted in the Aegean region was assuming an important function and becoming in its turn a fountain of new ideas. In each of these two regions culture advanced until in the last millennium B.C. it reaches the culmination that is typified for students in the names of Cyrus and Darius, the prophets of Israel, and the philosophers of Greece, as well as the teachings of the Buddha, Confucius, and Lao-Tse in those extensions of the agricultural civilization of the valley lands that grew up in the monsoon regions of Asia.

The rise of a region to the position of a fountain of new ideas is in every case accompanied by the evolution of cities and, whereas these near the Euphrates and the Nile may go back even to the fifth millennium B.C., it is in the third millennium that this notion spreads to the Aegean and that Hissarlik II, Orchomenos, Phylakopi, Knossos, Dhimini, Thermi, and other cities take their rise. They are followed by Mycenae and Tiryns in the second millennium, in the latter half of which Hissarlik revives as the Troy of legend, and Knossos eventually falls. Of the mainland Aegean cities of the second millennium B.C. a characteristic feature is the porched house or *megaron* already known at Dhimini and Hissarlik in early days but not occurring in Crete. It indicates a mixing of cultural streams in Greece and the Aegean that led on to the development of the classical cities, of which Athens and others had their origins in an earlier time.

In the last century B.C., and still more in the first century A.D., the function of spreading cultural ideas was to be taken over by Rome, the traditional date of the foundation of which is only 753 B.C. The city is clearly a much later feature in Italy than in Greece and the Aegean.

To spread the notion of the city was a complex matter; many different ideas, rituals, practices, and objects had to be carried simultaneously if collapse was to be avoided. Such ritual in early agricultural societies was usually bound to a particular spot, but we think that in the Bronze Age there came an increase of the power of abstract thought. We note the dissociation of the idea of Jahveh from a particular place or object, the ark, after the end of the Bronze Age among the Hebrews, and the ideas of Ikhn-aton in Egypt and Zoroaster or Zarathustra in Iran. Increases of intellectual power of this kind brought to Italy towards or after the end of the Bronze Age by Mycenean and Etruscan adven-turers escaping from the Achaean domination of the Aegean, were probably the main factors of the later astonishing change in the world situation of Italy. Ultimately what had been an out-lying area, with diverse cultures in different parts, became Roman with all that that term connotes in power and continuity. One reason for the delay in the spread of the city-idea westward is no doubt that small ships were cruelly buffeted, 'up and down in Hadria' as the account of Paul's voyage has it, and 'Scylla and Charybdis' in the straits of Messina were difficulties. Moreover, middle and south Italy did not naturally lend themselves to the early mixed farming, with cereals as the main resource, that we have seen spread from Asia Minor to the Danubian lands in the third millennium B.C., as described in Chapters 5 to 13 of *The Steppe and the Sown.* Thus Italy developed a village culture only in the north, as an extension of the peasant life on the Hungarian plain and among the Swiss lakes. The south of Italy, especially Sicily and Apulia, on the other hand, were, as we have seen in Chapters 1 and 3 of *The Way of the Sea*, in touch with the eastern Mediterranean at the end of the third millennium; Orsi thinks that there is evidence on several sites of a continuity of life down to far later periods, though this must not be held to imply continuity of overseas intercourse with the eastern Mediterranean. Along the east coast of Italy there are many hints of intercourse in the Bronze Age from the west of the Balkan peninsula, but along the west of Italy the indications of connexions with lands farther west still seem few and unimportant, as we should expect in view of the apparent decadence of the Iberian peninsula as the Bronze Age developed. There were many survivals of primitive peoples and their ways in cave fastnesses. When the Tuscan sources of copper and tin became known, the people of the Po basin spread southward and heralded large-scale movements of the Iron Age; these brought Illyrian peoples from the Balkan peninsula, probably around the north end of the Adriatic Sea, as well as other groups, and, as we think, gave rise to the peoples whose names we find at the dawn of History. The name *Italici* has been widely used for the Late Bronze Age peoples living in parts of the Po basin, but it is, perhaps, going a little too far to ascribe to them an Aryan language, though they came from the Danube, and the Danube had already received an influx of population from the steppe of south Russia as the latter dried up in the Bronze Age.

Our survey of Italy must consider more or less separately the north and the far south, including with the latter Sicily. Orsi has distinguished, following an early phase represented at Stentinello in east Sicily, a number of cultures that illustrate intercourse between Sicily and other Mediterranean lands. In Chapter 4 of *The Way of the Sea* we dealt with that of Villafrati

in west Sicily, which shows links with Spain in the occurrence
of beaker pottery, while that south-east Sicily made contacts
with the eastern Mediterranean is indicated by red-painted
pottery, rock-cut tombs with beehive-shaped interiors, and other
features. This 'First Siculan' phase is to be dated in the latter
half of the third millennium B.C. The Second Siculan phase was
characterized by the more general use of bronze; this phase grew
out of the first and was apparently for a long time a period of
minor importance, as we have suggested in Chapter 6 of *Merchant
Venturers in Bronze*. It is of some interest that tradition speaks
of the arrival of new influences in Sicily some time before the fall
of Troy, and it makes this immigration that of the Siculi; this
name is, however, used archaeologically for the sequence of
culture that began a thousand years or more earlier. Nevertheless there is no need to discard either tradition or archaeological
inferences, for we cannot but be impressed by the evidence for
expanded contacts with Mycenean civilization. The earlier
ossuary tombs of Siculan II, in which skeletons of large numbers
of persons were buried, apparently after the removal of the flesh,
became modified into tombs of smaller groups, probably
families, or even of individuals. Cremation, though the rule in
north Italy, was absent here. The cemeteries of the east coast
of Sicily have yielded a small amount of Mycenean pottery.
Simple early bronze weapons persist, but the winged bronze axe,
so important for this phase in north Italy, is quite scarce in the
island. Bronze lances and axes with shaft-holes, both related to
east Mediterranean cultures, are found, and apparently the latter
at least were made in Sicily.

The relationship with Mycenean Greece was still open to
doubt when Peet wrote his valuable book, but later finds of
*fibulae* reduce these doubts. Two-edged razors are a feature
of interest at this time. Orsi believes that they were introduced
into both south and north Italy from Mycenean Greece; type *b*

is very nearly the same as the Bronze Age razor-blade of north Italy. Bronze battle-axes in Sicily are another link with the eastern Mediterranean.

*Fibulae* with the simple bow, and others which have it elbowed, are known from both Sicily and south Italy. If they reached Sicily through south Italy, as is not impossible, we have a further item in which archaeo-logical data and tradition agree. The period concerned, more-over, is that following the fall of Knossos, when Mycenae and other centres were freed to spread their interests and activities over a wide region from Egypt and Libya to the Adriatic and from Sicily to Syria and the Euxine.

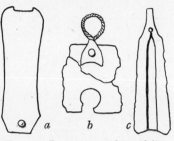

FIG. 37. Bronze razors from Sicily.

Reinecke says that in Italy, from Sicily northwards to the Alps and both east and west of the Apennines, there are Bronze Age graves and settlements, with early forms of *fibulae*, spreading from the south. He thinks the objects accompanying these *fibulae* in mainland Italy for the most part suggest dates after 1250 B.C., and he thinks it is earlier than the Villanova culture, which we shall have to discuss in our next volume. There occur here the *fibula* with simple bow, that with semicircular bow and that with elbowed bow, and some of the last have the pin-point holder lengthened; they are found mostly towards the south of mainland Italy. The *fibulae* of northern Italy often have the bow hammered out into an ornamental plate, spreading usually at right angles to the plane determined by the axes of the bow and the pin, as in an ordinary modern brooch. In this respect they differ from the *fibulae* of the Aegean and Hungary, where the complications added to the bow usually lie in the plane of those

H 2

two axes. This fact has been used by Myres to suggest that the
art of making safety-pins, though introduced from the Aegean
into north Italy through the south of that country, underwent a
special and independent evolution after their arrival.

In the previous chapter reference was made to the evolution
of the *fibula*, and one alternative mentioned was that in which
a thread was wound round the thorn or pin on both sides, with
the improvement effected by making in the pin-head a hole
through which to pass the thread. In the same chapter another
improvement, that in which the pin was bent, was discussed as
leading to the safety-pin all in one piece. But, if the thread were
replaced by a wire passed through the hole in the pin-head,
another type of *fibula*, in two pieces, would be evolved. One
piece would be the original pin, the other the wire hooked
through the hole and bent round at the other end to form a
catch for the pin-point. This two-piece *fibula* is very important
in north Italy, and Reinecke thinks it spread thence to south
Germany and the Baltic. Some writers would probably derive
the two-piece *fibula* more directly from that made in one piece,
but here we follow Myres's view.

In Chapter 5 of *Merchant Venturers in Bronze* we discussed at
some length the *Terremare* of north Italy; these are villages built
on piles with ramparts and ditches. They occur in the present
province of Emilia, chiefly between the Trebbia and the
Panaro, tributaries of the Po, and, to the north of that river, on
both sides of the Mincio. We have stated the general view that
the *Terremare* were the work of settlers who came into north
Italy from the Danube basin, but that the lake-dwellers of the
Alpine region also built pile-dwellings near Maggiore, Lugano,
Como, and, notably, Garda, on which last there occurs the oft-
quoted site at Peschiera. The older people of north Italy, often
known in archaeology with doubtful justification as the Ligures,
buried their dead, but the people of the *Terremare* practised

cremation. These latter separated eastern and western groups of their predecessors in north Italy, and the eastern group, in what was later the Romagna, seems to have borrowed a number of ideas from the *Terremare* people. The hut-villages of the older stock seem to have survived in use well into the Iron Age.

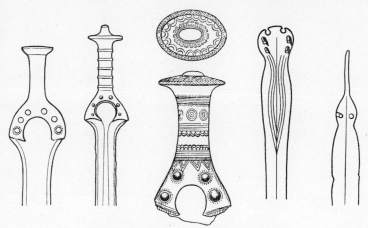

FIG. 38. Bronze swords from Italy.

As the *Terremare* represent a culture in essentials derived from Hungary, though with Alpine admixtures, we expect to find kinship in the swords of the two regions. There are early metal daggers with the hilt riveted on to the butt of the blade. Some of the north Italian swords show a hilt of this kind and, in one from the Bergamo district, the blade and hilt have been cast in one piece though the rivet-heads are retained for ornament. A few of the swords have an expanded butt with rivets, but no metal hilt at all; in some such cases the butt is richly ornamented. In others a knob at the end of the expanded butt may have represented, at first, merely the closing of the mould in which the sword was cast, but it is frequently developed into a longish tang, and swords of this type are known from Sicily as well as from the north. In the south such swords seem to be indications of links with Mycenean Greece, but in the north and east the suggestion is that their associations are with the Danube basin. There are also swords, especially in north and east Italy, in

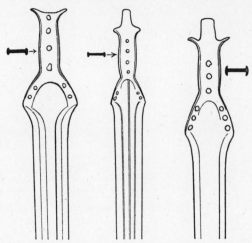

FIG. 39. Bronze swords from Sulmona, Trasimene, and Apulia.

which the hilt-tongue is flanged, as it is in so many from central Europe. An interesting group, found in the vicinity of Lake Fucino and Lake Trasimene, may possibly have come in by sea across the head of the Adriatic; its affinities are Hungarian.

There have been many discussions at various times concerning the Bronze Age influences of north upon south Italy. At Taranto has been found a settlement, one stage of which, belonging to the Bronze Age, showed huts on a wooden platform surrounded by a wall and moat. This led to its interpretation as a *Terramara* settlement. Much of the pottery of this settlement is, however, red south Italian ware quite different from that of the middle and north of the country; even if the *Terramara* culture had some influence here, the native element was clearly very strong, and it is perhaps going too far to assume that the wooden platform cannot have any other intrepretation than the one which ascribes it to *Terramara* influences. In middle and south Italy, moreover, there are indications at several sites of intercourse, during the Bronze Age, with the west of the Balkan peninsula across the Adriatic. Pottery with line and point incisions, often filled with white paste, has these features arranged to show the usual dog-tooth, chequer, spiral, and meander patterns, the last two being specially important. Similar pottery is known from Bosnia and elsewhere in the Balkans; on that side of the Adriatic it is more frequently found associated with remains of the pre-metal phase than is the case in Italy. This suggests that it is from the Balkan peninsula that this ware has come to eastern Italy.

This Balkan influence on Bronze Age Italy is of special interest in that it heralds a larger immigration from that region, probably in this case around the head of the Adriatic, as the Bronze Age passed into that of Iron, after the connexions with Mycenean culture had been discontinued.

#### BOOKS

PEET, T. ERIC. *The Stone and Bronze Ages in Italy* (Oxford, 1909).
CHILDE, V. GORDON. *The Bronze Age* (Cambridge, 1930).

## 9
## *West-Central and North-West Europe*

CHAPTERS 4 and 5 of our last volume dealt with the Early and Middle Bronze Age in central Europe. In the former the Bohemian Aunjetitz culture spread into Thuringia and parts of Bavaria, especially just south of the Danube; there was also a more western culture, best known from Adlerberg near Wörms, while some early hoards of bronze occur in the loess area of Rhenish Hesse. In the latter there spread along the hills of south Germany a culture characterized by burials on high places in low tumuli, sometimes scattered but often grouped together in numbers.

The tumuli are low, with the burials of individuals more or less in a circle around the edge and sometimes without a burial in the middle, though an interment of a specially important person may be noted there. Sauter found that often there was a primary burial covered with stones, and that around this other individuals were laid radially, together forming a circle; there might be a second circle around the first one. The bodies are often laid looking towards the centre. Sometimes the stones form a cist, sometimes there is a frame of single stones around each burial; this is usually a long rectangle or oval. Late in the development of this culture the custom of cremation was spreading, doubtless under the influence of the Urn-field people described below. When urns with cremated remains are buried in numbers in a tumulus, these urns may be set in circular frames and these circles usually follow one another around the circumference of the tumulus. Sometimes the collective burial is outlined by a zone of mixed stones and earth.

The people who made these burials had connexions with both the Aunjetitz and the western cultures just mentioned. The largest groups of graves are in Thuringia, on the Rhön and the Vogelsberg, near Darmstadt, near Hagenau in Alsace, in the Oberpfalz and Oberbayern, and on the Alb. There are also many finds of this period, as of early periods generally, in the basin behind Mainz. The tumulus culture does not extend far to the west of the German Rhine. The Thuringian group shows many examples of the use of the spiral ornament, a feature that associates it with developments in northern Europe to be discussed later.

The pins include some with wheel-heads and other related types, also some with disk or knob heads, the form known as the poppy-capsule head being found occasionally. Some swords have a typical flanged tongue with rivet-holes pierced as usual. Some

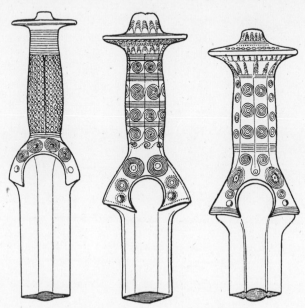

FIG. 40. Swords with octagonal hilts.

have no tongue of any kind but merely rivet-holes around the often expanded base of the blade. Some have a simple metal hilt like that of a dagger, fastened with two, three, or four rivets, the shoulder of the hilt being moulded around a semicircle or three-quarter circle cut out of its line of junction with the blade. The end of the hilt may be expanded into a flat or knobbed pommel. Most characteristic is the full-metal-hilted sword in which the hilt is octagonal, highly ornamented, with a knobbed pommel; this is known also in Italy and in Schleswig-Holstein and Scandinavia. That it spread northwards to the last-named region is almost certain, and it may have spread there from south Germany. Later variants of this sword in some cases have the hilt quadrangular. Baltic amber was obviously much prized

FIG. 41. South German Tumulus pottery.

by the Tumulus people of south Germany, who seem to have sent traders north for it, and so got it with very little admixture of features of the Baltic culture. Early Bronze Age trade may have been more direct than that of the middle period, which seems to have been an exchange from hand to hand, but in the Late Bronze Age long distance trade redeveloped. In addition to corded pottery of an early aristocratic element among the Tumulus people, there are several local styles of pottery, belonging no doubt to conquered peoples. Many pots are of pitcher form with a handle at the junction of the neck and body; some are undecorated, and in those that are ornamented both vertical and horizontal lines and points are employed, the vertical lines being rather commoner here than in many other cultures. There also occur warts or *mammae* already mentioned in Chapter 5 of *Merchant Venturers in Bronze* in connexion with early Lausitz pots. There is a good deal of indented or *Kerb-schnitt* ornament on the smaller vessels. Bronze axes include chiefly those with wings on either side near the base.

Late in the Bronze Age the Urn-fields culture, mentioned in Chapter 7, spread into south Germany. Its people had lowland villages but also fortified places on the hills, whereas their predecessors, of the Tumulus culture, lived on the hills and rarely made durable fortifications. The Tumulus culture with brown decorated pottery in the graves contrasts with the cremation cemeteries or urn-fields with their masses of undecorated pots. The newer culture restricted the older one and eventually influenced it, as at Bremelau, where one finds pitchers with a marked keel, as well as smaller cups. Urn-fields are numerous in the Frankfurt-Mainz basin of Rhine and Main, also near the Danube and south of Nürnberg, and they occur also in eastern France and Switzerland.

The earlier peasants of central Europe, as we have mentioned in Chapter 5 of *The Steppe and the Sown,* lived by hoe cultivation, made little use of domestic animals for labour, and occasionally moved their villages. Herding groups still more mobile probably dominated the peasants.

The Urn-fields culture inaugurates something akin to modern peasant life, very likely led or driven by a partly alien aristocracy of steppe-border origins. Villages became more durable, domestic animals probably helped in farm work, better horses were used, bread-wheat (*Triticum vulgare*) largely superseded the older varieties, and travelling smiths became a feature. The control of the sources of metal ores came to be very important. Increased use of grain seems to have involved, as usual, an increased demand for salt; probably the people by this time were also salting their meat; at any rate, they spread towards, and attached special importance to, salt-producing areas including the Jura and Hallstatt.

Switzerland lingered long in a late Neolithic phase, described in *Merchant Venturers in Bronze*, but received contributions from the early metal cultures of eastern France, Bohemia, and Hungary; this implies fairly easy intercourse in a dry, warm period.

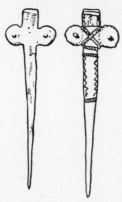

The people on the north side of the Alps were better able to penetrate those ranges than those on the south, to whom the sudden transition of climate, as they ascended the very sharp southern slopes, must have been very forbidding. Around the Swiss lakes were the pile-dwellings of peoples, who were probably refugees from the pressure of the early metal cultures. Most of these pile-dwellings were more or less deserted as the Bronze Age progressed, but some survived near the

FIG. 42.  Bronze Age pins from Jura and Aveyron, France.

mouths of lakes that were protected from floods by good gradients. The desertion of the pile-villages may have been due to the increasing melting of ice on the mountains as the climate grew warmer. An alternative view is that as the indigenous and intrusive cultures amalgamated there was no longer need for refuges. In the warm Late Bronze Age the lakes were low and pile-dwellings multiplied once more; prior to this, however, some people of the Tumulus culture, and others with the Urn-fields culture, and mixtures of both, came into the country. The older graves, chiefly in Valais, Ticino, Berne, and Fribourg, are all corpse burials, and their distribution and contents have been taken to indicate the advent of bronze-working into Switzerland from the west; this argument is largely based on the occurrence of a type of pin with circular wings at the sides of the head, found in south Germany, Switzerland, the French Jura, and in a megalithic monument in Aveyron. We suggested in Chapter 4 of *Merchant Venturers in Bronze* that the advance was from central Europe to southern France rather than in the opposite direction. The succeeding Tumulus culture, in any case, came from south Germany into north-east Switzerland and was followed by the Urn-fields culture with a late redevelopment of pile-dwellings, probably as the pressure of iron-using people began to make itself felt. The pile villages are numerous and yield many finds, because anything falling from the houses would drop among the piles and alluvium and would thus be preserved. Some of the bronze objects are of types belonging to the first phase of the Iron Age, the early Hallstatt period. Among the few iron objects known are some decorations on a bronze sword-hilt found at Mörigen, one bronze-hilted sword with an iron blade, a few fine pins at Zürich, and the plating of a number of arm-rings.

A sword which is found in many pile-villages has been named from that of Mörigen, though it has been generally supposed to have originated in eastern France and to be a feature introduced into the Swiss pile-dwellings. The biconical form of the grip-portion of the hilt, the shell-shaped pommel, the shape of the junction of the rivet and blade are all characteristic.

This type of sword does not occur in Italy, Hungary, or Denmark, and it is very rare in north-west Germany, though it did reach south Germany, Thuringia, Brandenburg, Pomerania, east Prussia, Finland, and Sweden. Some of the later varieties are described under the name of the Auvernier sword. These do not show the biconical grip, but have a lateral disk with rivets on the hilt. They are numerous in west Switzerland and originated either there or in south Germany, but, unlike the type mentioned previously, they spread especially to the Baltic. One should note

for comparison the relation mentioned above of the earlier
octagonal-grip sword to south Germany and the Baltic.

Another development from the Mörigen sword is the *Antenna*
sword, in which the pommel is drawn out on either side into

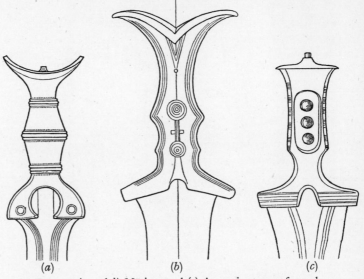

Fig. 43. (*a* and *b*) Mörigen and (*c*) Auvernier types of swords.

horns or *antennae* that may be spirally coiled. This type is
known over a wide area; it probably originated in eastern
France or Switzerland, but it occurs most often in north
Europe.

As characteristic of the Swiss pile-dwellings as their sword-
forms are their handled knives with curved edges to the blade,
their pins with pierced spherical, hollow heads, pins with a ring
and chain, pottery with bast fibres to help to bind it together,
and some gold. A famous golden bowl found at Zürich has sometimes been ascribed to the Late Bronze Age, but is better placed

in the Early Iron Age, to which period its decoration with animal figures clearly belongs.

Finds from the Swiss pile-dwellings are all the more numerous because they were submerged, as will be described later, and the remains were preserved in the deposits thus formed.

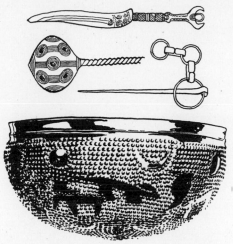

FIG. 44. Objects from the Swiss pile-dwellings.

The Late Bronze Age in Switzerland has been discussed as an extension of the culture of south Germany, and probably of east France as well, in the direction of the mountains during a relatively warm, dry period, and it has been said that it lingered on there after the introduction of iron.

The Baltic cultures of the Late Bronze Age may be discussed with analogous ideas in the background. This, it must be said at the outset, involves disagreement with the views of Kossinna and other archaeologists in Germany, who have thought that the west Baltic, or as they call it the Nordic region, had a brilliant autonomous development from the end of the Stone Age up to the development of the sword and its consequences. We agree rather with Sophus Müller and Reinecke, who think the West Baltic owed its remarkable evolution of culture in the Bronze Age to influences from outside, some sea-borne and others arriving by land. This point of view as regards the Late Stone Age and the Early Bronze Age has already been argued out in *The Way of the Sea* and *Merchant Venturers in Bronze*. One of the features of the Early and probably even of the Middle Bronze Age in central Europe was that in the Baltic region flint weapons were still made, with a remarkably skilled technique, to be placed with the dead, and also arrow-heads of very fine quality. It was not until the sword had come into use that the grave goods of that region began to include bronzes in any quantity. Both Müller and Reinecke date the rise of bronze culture in the north to the period when the Tumulus culture had spread to a considerable extent in south Germany, and they think its daggers, swords, and *fibulae* are derived, in the first instance, from imported ideas developed farther south. It is probable that the bronze culture in the Baltic had not gone far beyond preliminary stages before the general stirring of European life that occurred about 1300 B.C., as discussed in Chapters 7 and 8. Some of the hoards and stray finds of bronzes in the Baltic region, which include only early types of objects, may well be contemporary with the cultures that were still placing fine stone weapons in megalithic and 'single' graves, as described in Chapter 8 of *The Way of the Sea*. Religious conservatism as well as the rarity of metal may have helped the stone culture to survive in the north. Both megalithic and single-grave cultures may be emphasized once more here, because the one had maritime relations and other connexions with the south-east. The views here given are largely in agreement with those of Montelius, who, however, placed the dawn of the Bronze Age in the north at about 1700 B.C. This seems rather early, though some copper axes, which follow very closely the types in stone, may be as old.

One of the best known hoards which marks the coming of the bronze civilization into the Baltic lands is that of Galle-mose, on Laaland, Den-mark. This yielded eight bronze axes, of which three had rather distinct flanges while some of the others had indications of these. The lateral edges of these axes curve gently away from one another as they approach the cutting edge, and, in this respect, they are much like the early bronze axes of Brittany. Two of them, also, were decorated with a pattern of British type. In place of these two we give here another, also Danish, that shows this decoration very remark-ably executed. The hoard also contained nine heavy bronze rings, of which two

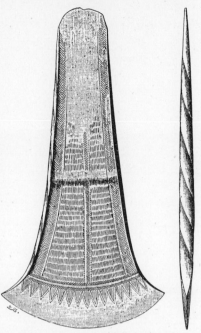

FIG. 45. Ornamented flanged axe.

were penannular, and three curious objects, which are supposed to be connected with the equipment of a horse.

Another hoard found at Pile in Scania, Sweden, confirms the inference made from that of Gallemose. It contains two flat axes and eleven with flanges, and one of the flat axes, which is very British in type, is the only bronze object in this hoard with a full complement of tin; the others are poor in this material.

One of the flanged axes shows indications of a stop-ridge. The hoard includes daggers with hilt and blade riveted together. Massive rings are found here again, and these are related to finds farther south. There is every reason to think of bronze coming into the Baltic area from both British and Bohemian directions. Though copper occurs near Gefle in Sweden and in the Glommen valley in Norway, it does not appear to be known that these sources of the metal were exploited in the Bronze Age; the metal was almost completely, if not entirely, imported, and Britain was a natural source of copper and tin, while Bohemia was famed especially for the latter. A recent discovery in the Shetlands, made by A. Curle, suggests that from these isles was obtained a certain amount of copper. It is possible that the massive rings mentioned above were metal bars in a form convenient for transport.

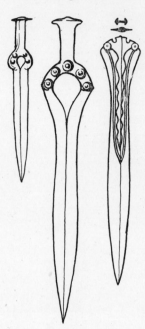

FIG. 46. Danish dagger and short swords.

Other objects from Scandinavia, generally believed to be of about the same or somewhat later age, and to belong to Sophus Müller's Period 2, and Montelius's early II, are a few socketed spear-heads from Uppland and Ostergötland, Sweden, and we note in passing that Gefle is near the former area; a bronze shaft-hole axe and a pin with spherical head both come from Zeeland in Denmark, as well as weapons of the dagger type, some of which have the blade lengthened to form a short sword. These weapons have a dagger hilt in metal riveted on to the blade. A halberd from Scania and a gold ring from Jutland are probably also early, but, whether this be so or not, the halberd seems to arrive earlier and to be more important in north Germany than in Denmark and Sweden.

The more advanced types of bronze finds in the West Baltic

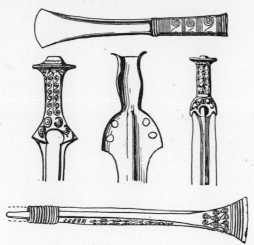

FIG. 47. Axes and swords from the Baltic area.

are for the most part to be dated from the period of activity beginning about 1300 or 1250 B.C., Sophus Müller's Period 3 onwards, when the life of Europe was stirred from the Aegean to the Baltic; the older finds show that, already before this great awakening, bronze had become more or less known over many parts of the region. In earlier phases the north German area naturally showed strong influences of the Aunjetitz culture, and cremation seems to come in sooner there than in Denmark or Scandinavia. Later on it is features of south German or north Italian culture that spread into north Germany and, in some cases, into Sweden and Denmark.

The beginnings of local bronze work show swords with hilts copied from dagger-hilts, and also swords with flanged tongues. Bronze battle-axes are also found with the hole, as in east-central Europe, prolonged into a tube at either end beyond the body of the axe, and often decorated with ribs or with engraved

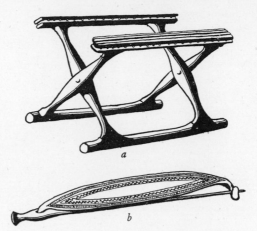

FIG. 48.  Camp-stool, and two-piece safety-pin.

patterns. *Fibulae*, some in one piece and some in two, are important as also are spiral arm-rings. The bronze axes show a special development of the flanged type achieved by lengthening the blade and by placing a metal band around part of the upper half to simulate the thread that bound the halves of the split stick-handle to the axis of the implement. There are also axes that have a socket as the basal half but keep the other half as a flanged blade; the difference between this and the socketed axe, discussed in Chapter 7 and mentioned later in this one, should be noted. In the peat here and there have been preserved wooden vessels, some with handles of the same material, boxes, and even very modern-looking camp-stools. Feminine personal adorn-

ment was much developed, the ornaments including amber
buttons with **V**-shaped boring, and gold ornaments using the
spiral design and recalling closely in some cases the corresponding

FIG. 49.  *Tutulus.*

objects from the Mycenean civilization of Greece and no doubt
derived ultimately from that source. A special ornament was
the *tutulus*, a spiked disk worn in the waist girdle and usually
richly engraved. The latter part of this phase of rising local
industry is separated off from the earlier by Müller as a third
period because of the beginning of indigenous designs in the
local industry, the *tutuli* being a most notable feature.

Once begun, the local development of bronze industry took

great strides during Sophus Müller's fourth period or the end of Montelius's Period II.   As horses, battle-axes, and richly ornamented sword-hilts are among the great features, there seems to

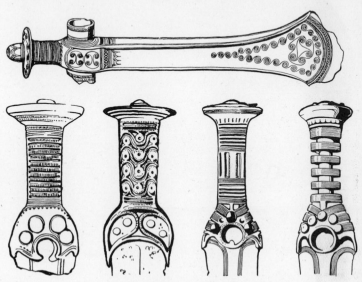

Fig. 50.   Battle-axe and swords.

have been an increase in trade with the continental interior, doubtless especially with the tin regions of Bohemia, perhaps also with the copper-producing regions in Slovakia, where the battle-axe had been the chosen weapon of horsed warriors, as we have seen in Chapter 7.   By this time the amber trade route had become very important and the sword with a fully metallic octagonal hilt reached the Baltic from south Germany.   A famous object of this period is a bronze horse modelled as if it were drawing a splendidly ornamented bronze disk, both being mounted on wheels, and originally probably entirely covered with gold leaf.   Others include spirally ornamented *fibula*-heads, tweezers, and razors with holders shaped like horses' heads. Two clothed figures have been recovered from the peat and are shown both as actual specimens and in restored form in the Copenhagen Museum; the blanket-stitching binding the edge of the cloth is still clearly visible. For some reason pottery, which had been

FIG. 51. Bronze horse and disk.

such a feature of the end of the Stone Age in Denmark, was of less account in the Bronze Age.

As the industry grew older, during Montelius's Period III or Sophus Müller's 5 and 6, towards 1000 B.C., sword-hilts became more elaborate, some having disks of perishable material alternating with those of bronze. Cauldrons on wheels, glass beads, gold wire, and fine ornaments are found. A bent sword of Egyptian origin has been described, also square socketed axes of the type mentioned in Chapter 7. At this time the east of modern Germany was becoming more important, mainly showing an extension of the west Baltic area's culture towards the Vistula.

At the end of this phase, not far from 1000 B.C., old-time

patterns died out, the influences of Mycenean Greece finally
disappeared and sword-hilts showed revolutionary alterations of
style. The Urn-fields culture reached north Germany but

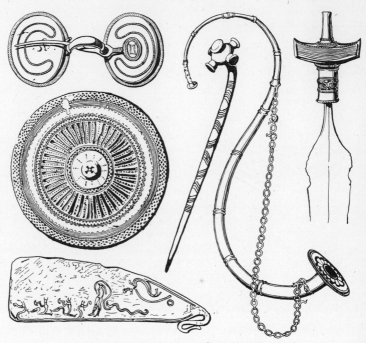

Fig. 52.  Late Bronze Age objects from Denmark.

apparently the tumulus persisted in Scandinavia, even where
cremation became the rule.   East Germany seems to have had
more cists.

At Seddin a grave with corbelled roof and burnt remains
contained a number of vessels including an Italian one of bronze.
There was much gold imported, a hoard at Eberswalde having
yielded 2·5 kilograms of the metal.   This period is called by

Müller the beginning of the Later Bronze Age of the north. It shows influences of the iron-using Hallstatt culture, that had at this time developed at a famous source of salt supplies in the north-east Alpine valleys. This is seen especially in what are called spectacle-*fibulae* and in the new artistic conceptions that decorate the knife-blades. Some famous musical instruments like trumpets are thought to date from this phase. After this, elaborately ornamented disks and vessels were still made for some time, and there are copies in bronze of types of objects made in

Fig. 53.   Rock drawings from Sweden.

iron farther south, just as at the dawn of the Metal Age there were copies in stone of types of objects known in copper or bronze in the same direction. The great days were over and a decline had set in that cannot but be paralleled with that of the Swiss pile-dwellings. This decline will be discussed in a later chapter.

Sweden and parts of Norway are rich in rock drawings. Of these some are naturalistic and, whatever their date, represent the tradition of the hunter artists of the later part of the Old Stone Age, described in *Hunters and Artists*. Often they occur on cave or rock faces in positions which suggested that they were chipped from boats when the sea-level was higher than it ever is now. Other drawings are schematized men, women, ploughs, and boats, and by a number of more or less circumstantial arguments, including the drawings of weapons, these are generally thought to belong to the Bronze Age, when Denmark and south Sweden developed an agricultural civilization while apparently the hunting and fishing life persisted farther north. Denmark has only a few drawings, on loose blocks. Northern Bohüslan is their chief home, but they are also known near Norrköping and in Uppland. They are rarely found in or near graves, which lie on the hills or cliffs, but rather near the arable lands. One should compare with these drawings the pictures graven on Bronze Age razors.

An outstanding feature of the Late Bronze Age in the Baltic area is the great vigour of local ideas and the relative absence of direct influence from the Lausitz and Urn-fields cultures in this region, though these cultures had much indirect bearing on the evolution sketched out above. The Baltic area, like Switzerland and, as we shall see in the next chapter, Atlantic Europe, shows a distinct lag in the Bronze Age when compared with the Aegean.

## 10

## *Atlantic Europe*

IN *The Way of the Sea* the opening of a great period of activity in Atlantic Europe was discussed. As the Bronze Age advanced, that activity continued but with modifications due to the decline in importance of Iberian tin-bearing sands, exhaustion of the impulse of the Beaker-making people, increase in importance of the Continental interior as Bohemian tin came into trade, and probably the occurrence of warm summers making Spain very dry but the west Baltic more prosperous.

Ireland, important for gold, applied ideas of pottery decoration, partly derived from the Iberian peninsula, to pots of local type such as the Food-vessel. The persistence of these local types of pottery and the absence of *fibulae* in the British Late Bronze Age, in spite of intrusions of new types of weapons from the Continent, suggest that bands of warriors were immigrating without their women, or perhaps many craftsmen. Breton pots, described and figured in Chapter 2 of *Merchant Venturers in Bronze*, apparently continued in use in west Britain. Some of the cinerary urns of Britain lend themselves to comparison with those of Pyrenean France as well as with some from south Holland, but the associations of the latter suggest a rather later time. Some years ago R. C. C. Clay rescued a few urns from a

FIG. 54. Food-vessels.

Late Bronze Age urn-field at Pokesdown, Hampshire, and he is able to relate these to some from other places in south England as well as to specimens from southern and eastern France. Pottery with applied ribs of clay marked by finger-tip impressions is a feature of the Late Bronze Age in England, and this type of ornament was of old standing in central Europe. In Britain it is called the Deverel-Rimbury type.

In the *Antiquaries Journal*, Fox has recently discussed a type of earthenware ornament moulded in clay applied to the pot; this style is characteristic of Ireland, the Welsh coast, the north of England, and parts of Scotland. Comparing this with the distribution of food-vessels, one is tempted to suggest that the encrusted, or, better, *appliqué*, pots represent an idea spreading from Ireland.

In Chapters 5 and 6 of *Merchant Venturers in Bronze*, the bronze axe of the Middle Bronze Age, commonly called the palstave, was discussed in some detail. It may well be that it persisted into later times, and that some of the hoards in Atlantic lands, in which the palstave is the most advanced type of axe, belong nevertheless to a time near the end of the Bronze Age.

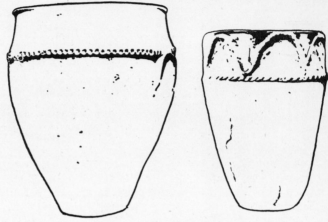

FIG. 55. British cinerary urns.

The numbers of hoards of this kind in western and north-western France, including Brittany, and the abundance of this type of axe in Britain, at any rate support the idea of continued intercourse with west France and Brittany which has been urged above in the study of pottery. Palstaves with two side-loops instead of the ordinary single one are known, as Crawford has shown, from the west of the Iberian peninsula, western France, south England, and Ireland.

Estyn Evans has recently analysed several facts connected with bronze axes and swords in Switzerland, France, and Britain, and has shown that the winged axe came west in Gaul even more abundantly than was suggested in Fig. 34 of *Merchant Venturers in Bronze*. It is the winged axe with the wings at the base, called by German scholars the *Lappenabsatzbeil*, and it seems to have originated in the west Alpine region as a hybrid between the palstave and the axe with median wings. In general in western Europe the winged axe played a much smaller part than the socketed one to be discussed below, but Evans has shown that

FIG. 56. Deverel-Rimbury urns.

this is not everywhere the case. In the Morbihan, Brittany, in the Late Bronze Age, the winged axe is three times as abundant as the socketed one, and, associated with the winged axe in Brittany, one finds a socketed axe with wings cast in relief near the mouth of the socket. This particular variety also occurs in western Switzerland. There are also various small objects found in hoards in both regions. The discovery of moulds for the manufacture of end-winged axes in north-west France is held to show that these objects spread west not merely as obsolete material to be re-cast, but as part of a culture, under the influence of which the metallurgical industry became more varied than it had previously been in that region.

In discussing, in Chapter 9, the pile-dwellings of the Late Bronze Age in Switzerland, the suggestion has been made that they date from the period when the iron-armed peoples were beginning to press upon the bronze culture. The pressure may well have led to a movement, whether of large groups or only of craftsmen and their culture, from Switzerland and its borders to the ancient centre in south Brittany, which was obviously still important. South-eastern Britain was affected as well, and the importance of the Bayeux region, the Somme, and most of all the lower Seine suggests possible lines of connexion. In Britain it is especially the Thames estuary and the coasts of Sussex and Kent that are important for finds of this kind.

The socketed axe is one of the most abundant of prehistoric metal objects, many thousands having been found in west Normandy in the department of Manche, and in north and west Brittany in the departments of Côtes-du-Nord and Finistère. They are of fairly frequent occurrence in Morbihan, but the number there is far less than in Manche or Côtes-du-Nord or Finistère. The same is true of the departments around the Seine estuary. Hoards with socketed axes are very scarce in south-west France and in the north-east as well. The impression given is that of an industrial idea being brought to north-west France, and of its great development and probably long continuance in that region. A group of hoards in the departments of Aude, Hérault, and Tarn, though not large, is worth mentioning; very few have been found in interior departments. Some of the Norman and Breton socketed axes are so thin as to be of little value as tools, and the suggestion has been made that they were either votive objects, charms, or forms of currency; these ideas are strengthened by the fact that a few of the Breton hoards contain axes made of copper, tin, and lead, and some are quite miniature. In a woman's grave of immediately pre-Roman or Roman date at Arras there was found a socketed axe one inch long: it was obviously an amulet. Heathery Burn Cave in the county of Durham has yielded an important hoard of the Late Bronze Age. It includes jet and one amber bead, and what are apparently imports related to the amber-trade routes. Among

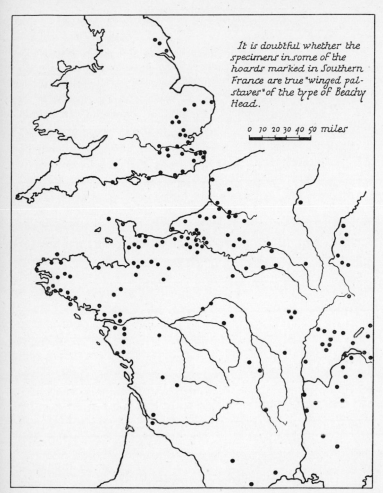

It is doubtful whether the
specimens in some of the
hoards marked in Southern
France are true "winged palstaves" of the type of Beachy
Head.

0  10  20  30  40  50  miles

FIG. 57. Map showing the distribution of winged axes in France and England.

these imported types of objects is a bronze bucket-urn, resembling a few others from Ireland, England, and north-west Europe; this is thought to be derived from the Italian culture of that country's Early Iron Age. It affords an indication of the lagging of Britain behind other regions in cultural evolution. A socketed bronze axe containing a large proportion of lead invites comparison with the Breton specimens mentioned just above, and a bronze sword of similar composition was also found. A hoard at Brécy in the department of Aisne included a large number of fragments of socketed axes, sickles, spear-heads, and other objects, obviously intentionally broken; the fragments were said to be all of very much the same weight, and this has been thought to point to the currency theory. It is doubtless important that, common as the socketed axe is in hoards in Brittany and Britain, such axes are very rare in burials. One hoard in Côtes-du-Nord has yielded 4,000 axes linked by metal wires, and one in Manche yielded 8,000. Outside these two departments and Finistère the hoards hardly ever contain axes in hundreds. Hoards of this period here and there in other departments have the axes linked up by bronze wire.

Some such axes have the socket cylindrical, in others it is octagonal, and in many, especially in Brittany, it is square in section; some, especially of the last, are ornamented with ribs or triangles, or with circles or knobs, but these are a feature of north-west France and Britain, not of Switzerland. There is usually a loop near the socket-mouth through which to pass the cord binding the axe-head to its handle.

In Chapter 7 the opinion was expressed that the socketed axe had evolved in the Lausitz region. It is not very common in Switzerland and it may well be that it reached north-west France not from the eastern part of that country but from farther north.

For Great Britain we may hope to gain much more exact knowledge when the Catalogue of Bronze Age implements now nearly completed has been studied and detailed distribution-maps have been made. At the moment it seems that the bearers of socketed axes came chiefly to the east coast and up the inlets and rivers that afforded entrances farther into the country; the special types of socketed axe that were developed in Brittany and

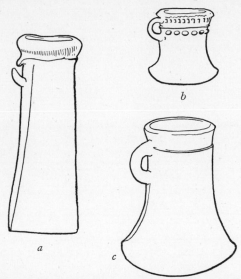

FIG. 58. Socketed axes from (*a*) Alfriston, (*b*, *c*) Ireland.

west Normandy occur in Cornwall, Dorset, and other parts of south England. It is possible that raw material went from south-west Britain to north-west France, and it is certain that, quite late in the Bronze Age, there was an export of these axes to south England. In Ireland the socketed axe developed a much-expanded edge, as if it were hammered out, probably again and again.

One of us has made special studies of bronze swords and these have been supplemented by Estyn Evans's article in *Antiquity*,

1930. Without repeating here minute details of the discussion of sword types, it may be said that there is agreement among many workers as to the spread of some leaf-shaped bronze swords from Switzerland and eastern France to north-western France and south-eastern and eastern England along with the winged axe.

The spread of related types of sword to Ireland and to the Atlantic portions of the Iberian peninsula is noteworthy. There is probably some correlation with the Deverel-Rimbury pottery noticed above.

Scotland has yielded a number of swords which are related to those of Ireland, and, as some have been found in the Hebrides, this suggests a maritime spread northward, perhaps analogous to the later one of the Scots. There may be a relation between the distribution of these swords and that of the *appliqué* pottery discussed above.

The complexity of inter-regional culture exchanges at this time is greater than anything known from earlier periods, and indicates abundantly the increasing difficulty of applying the methods used in this series as later and later phases of cultural evolution come to be treated. There are everywhere indications of long-distance communication, of exchange of ideas, of the copying of models brought from afar, of local elaboration of design, in short of the activity of reflective thought among the craftsmen of the time.

In view of the complexities just mentioned it will be of value to add here a short summary concerning each of the main regions discussed in this chapter.

Near Bonn the Rhine emerges from the deep cleft it has sawn through the re-uplifted block of old and worn mountains that form the Eifel and Ardennes on the west and the mountains of middle Germany to the east. Terraces of the river which have been narrow in the cleft broaden out as the Rhine reaches the plains, and on these terraces a Bronze Age culture developed with contributions from the Tumulus peoples, and later the Urn-field peoples, the former mainly from south and mid-Germany, the latter from the same regions and probably from areas farther north as well, while, in the background, are

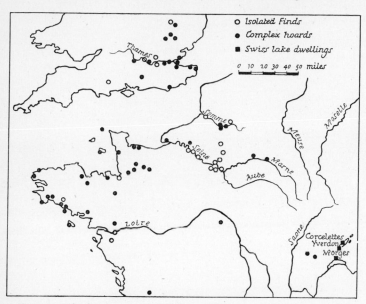

Fig. 59. Distribution of swords, Beachy Head type. Sides almost parallel, sometimes with narrowed point; midrib rounded and outlined by lateral incised lines, deep squarish notches at base of blade, broad tang. The sword also occurs on numerous sites around the Atlantic coast of the Iberian Peninsula.

inheritances from the makers of corded ware and of both corded and bell beakers. Mound-graves are found on the edges of river terraces; those of the later Bronze Age contain mostly cremated remains. The Urn-field people mostly utilized the lower terraces and their urn-fields are not on the terrace-edge. As the Bronze Age passed into that of Iron, the Urn-fields culture spread its influence among the people of the mound-graves. Broadly, the Low Countries go with the Rhenish culture just mentioned, and both have evidence of fairly early connexion with west Baltic cultures. Great Britain seems to have had an increase of population; there was traffic across it to and from Ireland, and its pottery suggests links with the south and east. Socketed axes and swords indicate the arrival of immigrants; these occupied the water-meadows of the eastern rivers and the riverine lowlands generally, at least where they were free from woods on clay soils.

While Ireland and Scotland show indications of intercourse with Europe, they are to some extent distinguished by the development of native fashions, as Fox and others have shown. Western France received from Switzerland and Burgundy an impetus in bronze-work, represented by winged axes and some types of swords. The socketed axe may have come to it by a more northerly route; in west Normandy and Brittany, especially north and west, it became the main object of an industry that seems to have used ores from Britain and exported thither some of its finished products. The south of France was apparently affected chiefly by Burgundy and Switzerland. The Iberian peninsula had apparently lost much of its ancient importance by the middle of the Bronze Age; later on it received a fresh impetus along its Atlantic shores from farther north, and, at Huelva, objects demonstrating that connexion are found with others of western Mediterranean character.

The movements and changes of civilization in the Late Bronze Age in western and west-central Europe, at least, and probably in the Mediterranean as well, are related to climatic alterations that—because we are here discussing a period well after 1000 B.C.—we must mention in dealing with the topics of this chapter, in order to keep together data of the Late Bronze cultures, though there is inevitably a lag in time between central

Europe on the one hand and the British Isles, Switzerland, or the Baltic on the other.

The climatic change has been studied in much detail through the method of counting the pollen grains in various old soil accumulations. In the older ones, provisionally linked with the Bronze Age, 30–60 per cent. of the pollen grains are of oak, lime, and elm and related trees. In recent ones the pollen grains of this group of trees are only 5–15 per cent. at the most, and this only in favourable situations near the sea and so on. The beech- and fir-trees have gained at the expense of the older forests which were rich in trees that demanded warmer summers and could stand drought better than the more sensitive beech. There is also evidence of moorland bogs growing at the expense of ancient forests.

Further, while a good many details are still not clear, it is probable that the land lay deeper in the sea in the earlier and warmer period than in the cooler one which followed it. A rise of the land in the Scandinavian area may thus have been a factor of the climatic change which is described by Munthe on the basis of investigation of water-snail shells as the change from the *Litorina* to the *Limnaea* period. *Litorina* is a marine, *Limnaea* a freshwater form.

Another factor of the situation has been suggested by Pettersson. He has found mathematically that there are secular variations of the strength of tides, and that these were at a minimum about 1200 B.C. and at a maximum about 350 B.C. Stronger tides, Brooks has argued, mean more interference with the northern ice edge, more ice floating out into the ocean, more cyclonic disturbances, less summer warmth and so on. The transition from a period of warmth about 1200 B.C. to a cold time some centuries later may well have been influenced by this tidal change. In several parts of Germany there are two layers of peaty material with *sphagnum* moss in it as indications of wet phases of climate. The later of these two apparently began to grow at about the time suggested above for the change in temperature and rainfall under discussion. It is widely agreed that the Late Bronze Age pile-dwellings of Switzerland ended their history through a calamitous rise of lake levels, and that river erosion became more active in several places. Gams and Nordhagen have suggested that the cool and wet phase made glaciers grow. Other physiographical studies in Bavaria suggest that at this time some new lakes appeared and that the land here was sinking meanwhile. In some areas loess and blown sand became covered with vegetation, even trees, as, for example, near Lake Constance. It is also claimed that at this time ice reoccupied some areas in the Alps which had formerly been clear enough for human movement and intercourse as witnessed by various finds.

We must not go too far beyond the limits of the subject of this chapter, but it is important to point out that, contemporary with these changes in the west and north-west of Europe, there was apparently the change in the Russian steppe from its Bronze Age condition approaching emptiness to its activities of the Scythian phase. There were also movements, one after another, into Spain, which apparently woke up again after its phase of lessened activity in the dry and warm period. These indications make it likely that the classical lands of the Mediterranean at this time enjoyed some increase of rainfall, and here Myres is of the same opinion; the Hebrew records indicate a contemporary increase of agriculture in Palestine. The changes thus argued for west and north-west Europe, and dated perhaps 850 B.C., with a century or so on either side left very doubtful, were probably changes that further research will show to have affected many parts of the world.

CHILDE, V. GORDON. *The Bronze Age* (Cambridge, 1930).
BROOKS, C. E. P. *The Evolution of Climate*, 2nd ed. (London, 1925).
FOX, CYRIL. *The Personality of Britain* (Cardiff, 1932).
PEAKE, HAROLD. *The Bronze Age and the Celtic World* (London, 1922).

# 11

## The Monsoon Lands of Asia

IN our last volume we described the movements of the people of the eastern steppe, who spoke Indo-European dialects; we showed how they wandered over north Persia and Turkistan and that at about 1500 B.C. they divided owing to religious differences, the majority remaining in Turkistan, while some passed through the mountains to settle in the Punjab.

We know little of those remaining in Turkistan, who are known as Iranians, for the legends that have been handed down, and were subsequently embodied in the epic of Firdausi, give us no reliable information, though we gather from them that these tribes were constantly at war with others, called Turanian, who are believed to have been Mongols. At the close of the period with which this volume deals, about 1000 B.C., tradition tells us of a king, whose name has been handed down as Kaiomurs, who was ruling at Balkh over an Iranian tribe afterwards known as the Persians.

Of those that entered India, who are known as the Aryans, we know a little more, though our information is still very imperfect. Our scanty knowledge is gleaned from the collection of hymns, known as the Rig-veda; most of these hymns are believed to have been composed between 1200 and 1000 B.C., though some may be earlier, and from these it has been conjectured that the Aryan tribes were settled in the Punjab by 1400 B.C., if not before, though it seems unlikely that any of them had arrived in the land of the five rivers before 1700 B.C.

From the earlier hymns we can form a fairly clear picture of the district that their authors occupied. It was bounded on the north by the Himalayas, which they knew as the Himavant Mountains. On the west they were in touch with the Kabul river, and they were familiar with the Indus, though probably only with its upper waters. On the east they had reached the Sarasvati, which flows between the Sutlej and the Jumna, while one reference is found to the Ganges, though it is thought that they had not then entered its valley. It is believed that they had not spread farther south than the point at which the Indus receives its main tributaries, though the word *samudra*, which

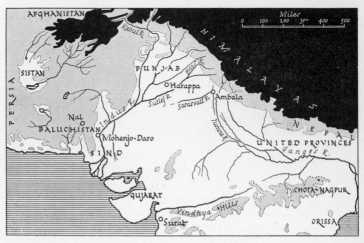

FIG. 60. Map of the Punjab.

at a later date signifies the ocean, occurs more than once in the hymns; it has been conjectured, however, that this word refers to the lower reach of the Indus, which is there so wide that from a small boat in the centre it is impossible to see either bank. This part of the Indus is still called by the natives the 'Sea of Sind'.

In view of Sir John Marshall's recent discoveries of an older civilization in India, we are able in some measure to contrast the incoming Aryans with the peoples of the older cultures in that country. Mohenjo Daro, a few miles below the site of the great modern barrage in Sind, apparently came to an end before the Vedic period, and Marshall thinks that the remains of the city so far uncovered date from between 3250 and 2750 B.C. Harappa lies 400 miles farther north in the Punjab, and the same writer believes it began earlier and lasted later than the southern city.

Frankfort has recently published a description of a seal found in the desert about fifty miles north-east of Bagdad, at Eshnunna, which may well have been on a land route eastward from

FIG. 61. Impression of seal from Eshnunna.

Mesopotamia through the Zagros range towards many lands, among which the Indus region may have been one. He has stated that 'the convention in which the feet and ears and the folds in the elephants' skin are represented' and 'the peculiar rendering of the ears of the rhinoceros' 'recur identically on seals from Mohenjo Daro'. He argues that we have here an importation from the Indus valley, which from evidence on the site reached Eshnunna about 2500 B.C. There are other importations which give general confirmation to this inference. The date is of interest as supporting Marshall's view that the Indus civilization continued, at any rate at Harappa, after the decline of Mohenjo Daro.

The people of this old culture were irrigators dependent on the annual flood of the Indus, and in that period Sind was apparently far less arid than it is now. They grew wheat, barley, and cotton of a coarse type, had short-horned cattle, zebus, water-buffaloes, camels, and sheep as well as pigs and fowls; there is some doubt about their possession of horses. They used carts and chariots, and made stone vases as well as wheel-turned pottery. Their metal-work was elaborate, but tin was obviously very scarce. They also had important commercial relations with Mesopotamia through Baluchistan as well as by sea. Their large cities contained houses built of kiln-baked bricks and roofed with timber balks.

It would be going far beyond the evidence available to suggest that Marshall's discoveries give us the basis of what may be called Dravidian India. At the same time, however, they may well be held to show us one of the chief factors of the civilizations that the Aryans found on their arrival in India, and among those civilizations the Dravidian languages were apparently widely used. It is a possible hypothesis that, through connexion with Mesopotamia in very early times, the art of irrigation arrived in India, and thence cultivation spread over the peninsula, to be modified in both its material and social implications when rice came into use.

The Aryans were village-dwellers who, like others around the great steppe, took refuge at times in forts. They had cattle and *yava*, probably barley, and they used a plough drawn by bulls; the name of this implement in both Indian and Iranian is based on the word *krish*, so we know it was common to both groups before they separated. They used spears, swords, axes, slings, and especially the bow. The possession of the sword suggests a date not earlier than the middle of the second millennium B.C. They had horses, cattle, sheep, and goats, and sacrificed the horse, which was a sacred animal. They were great meat-eaters like the Achaeans, and like them also they despised a fish diet. Gaming with dice, horse-racing, chariot-fighting, lion- and buffalo-hunting were among their pastimes. Their earlier rite of burial eventually gave place to cremation, a widespread phenomenon in the later part of the second millennium B.C. Their gods were Dyaus, the sky god, Prithivi, the earth mother, Varuna, Mitra, Indra, the storm god, and Agni, the sacred fire. They did not know the tiger of the Ganges basin nor had they tamed the elephant.

From a comparison of the two cultures one gets a contrast between traders and cultivators of the older culture and warrior herdsmen of the newer, and evidence of an old civilization, doubtless in a state of decay, apparently over-run by vigorous barbarians, as happened in many other cases, and as seems to be suggested by some episodes in the Mahabharata. It is quite likely that the higher social grades among the conquered may have been admitted into some relation with the conquerors, and this is one possible origin of the Vaiçya group or caste, though these may have been the cultivators among the Aryans before the latter reached India.

The settlement of the Aryans seems speedily to have transformed the Kshatriya or Warrior caste into a number of Rajput clans attached to local fortresses. The analogies with the Achaeans are remarkable.

The Brahmanas or Brahman caste raises difficult problems. They have become the dominant caste in civil life in India, but their outlook is very different from that of the Aryan invaders. They regard the cow as sacred and are not eaters of meat as were the earlier Aryans.

Indian literature possesses two great epics, the Mahabharata and the Rāmāyana, both of which were compiled many centuries later, though they draw pictures of the Vedic period or the time that immediately followed it. Embedded in the Rāmāyana are a number of stories relating to events that are clearly much older, and one of these seems to have an important bearing on the problem that we are discussing. It relates how a body of Kshatriyas fought against a Brahman with a view to capturing a wonderful cow. In spite of their prowess in arms, they were unable to stand against the magic exercised by the Brahman, who succeeded in retaining his beast. This story may, of course, be merely a moral tale to illustrate the superiority of religious over physical force, but it is possible that it signifies a clash in the very distant past between two groups, involving a fight in which the weaker of the two had gained the upper hand by artifice and the exercise of magical threats. An alternative suggestion is that the Brahmanas represent and continue the priestly element of the older civilization resurging as old civilizations are so apt to do. The resurgence of the English in Plantagenet times is a case in point.

Under these three great groups or castes of the so-called twice-born, Brahmanas, Kshatriyas, and Vaiçyas were the native serfs or Çudras. We thus gain a picture of the basis of caste in India, an institution aiming at the protection of an intrusive culture in danger of submergence under an immense indigenous mass reduced to servitude. Caste has become complicated in many ways. Occupational groups are the most important, but groups associated with localities, with rites and ceremonies and so on are continually added. Castes are always growing or decaying, raising their social status or losing it. The complexities of caste reach a high-water mark in the United Provinces, where the intermingling of conquerors and conquered must have been specially intimate, as here the conquerors, advancing forestwards from the west across successive rivers, had to divide and come to terms with the natives.

The Vedic hymns of the Aryans tell of some of the battles in their victorious movement into India. The most famous of these was that fought on the banks of the rivers Vipāç and Çutudrī, the modern Beās and Sutlej, by the Bharatas, under Sudās their king, against ten allied tribes. This, known as the battle of the ten kings, is thought to have taken place about 1100 B.C.

In our last volume we carried the history of China down to the year 1122 B.C., when Wu-wang established himself upon the throne as the first emperor of the Chou Dynasty. With the advent of this dynasty China entered upon a period of prosperity.

FIG. 62. A bronze dating from the Chou Dynasty.

The first emperor, usually known as the Warlike Prince, has received unstinted praise from all historians since the time of Confucius, who considered him a most exemplary ruler and a model to be followed by those that came after. During his reign embassies arrived from the kings of Korea and Cochin China, and the emperor established his frontiers so firmly that there was little trouble during the succeeding reigns, under which good rule and prosperity continued. Chinese history tells us little of the deeds of most of these emperors, but has much to say of Mu Wang, who reigned from 1001 to 946 B.C. This emperor introduced the system of redeeming offences by the payment of fines, thereby paving the way for much bribery and corruption, which has been rampant ever since in the Middle Kingdom.

The country at this time seems to have consisted of a number of semi-independent states loosely held together by fealty to the emperor, but liable to break up into fractionated parts should the influence of the monarch decline. Civilization forged ahead under the emperors of this dynasty, and from this time date a small number of beautiful bronzes that are to be seen in some of our museums.

BOOKS

*The Cambridge History of India*, vol. i (Cambridge, 1922).
BENJAMIN, S. G. W. *Persia* (London, 1889).
SYKES, P. M. *History of Persia*, vol. i (London, 1915).
GRISWOLD, H. D. *The Religion of the Rigveda* (Oxford, 1923).
MARSHALL, SIR JOHN. *Mohenjo Daro and the Indus Civilization* (London, 1932).
HIRTH, F. *Ancient History of China* (New York, 1908).

12

# General Summary

AN age, characterized by so much complexity in the movements and inter-relations of peoples as that surveyed in this book, could not be treated primarily in its separate regions. It has thus happened that much of the chronological sequence, which usually occupies the last chapter in the volumes of this series, has already been given in earlier chapters. Here, therefore, the attempt will be made to sketch as general a view as possible of the world of man during the latter half of the second millennium B.C., and to note some of the greater influences that were driving it through the earlier phases of the most important revolution in the whole story of mankind.

*Merchant Venturers in Bronze* showed that metal had become a fairly widespread and common feature in the life of large parts of the northern hemisphere of the Old World, while the poverty or absence of a Bronze Age in intertropical Africa was a feature of outstanding importance, indicative of the isolation of that region from the main currents of civilization.

Struggles in the Aegean region had left the island of Crete as a trading centre in a triumphant position, with its palace civilization, luxury, and art, apparently dependent on a large amount of slave labour. The island's position not only favoured maritime commerce, but protected the traders' home for a time from the onset of steppe-land warriors, who at that period were conquering far and wide. The great northern steppe, as we have seen in the *Steppe and the Sown*, was apparently occupied in early days by very long-headed peoples, whereas in subsequent ages it has had broad-headed inhabitants. This seems to be one of the few cases known of a replacement of one population by another. In *Merchant Venturers in Bronze* reference was made to the outpouring of warriors from the steppe into India and Europe, and probably into China as well, and also to analogous movements affecting Mesopotamia and Egypt. One hypothesis advanced to interpret these movements suggests that this was a period of warmth and drought, and that it was aridity that drove the peoples out of the steppes. Another suggestion is that they had acquired the use of the horse and that, when they had combined this with a knowledge of metal, their power of conquering and organizing settled cultivators was immensely increased. It is probable that there is a measure of truth behind both views of the matter. In support of the second suggestion there is the evidence of the spread of the horse into India, Mesopotamia,

Egypt, and Europe. In support of the former hypothesis there is the negative evidence of the absence of discoveries dating from this period in the steppe regions, in which those belonging to the third millennium B.C. are so important.

The advent of the horse into Egypt seems to be associated with a change in the character of that country from that of a self-contained economy to that of the widespread empire, with strong military and commercial activities, that developed under Hatshepsut and Thutmose. The consequent exchanges of thought, led on, apparently, to the famous attempt of Ikhn-aton to found a universal religion, that was to replace the old rituals, based on the desire to ensure fertility. After the super-activity and expansion of the military and commercial effort, came intensive thought, with its effects of disruption and fatigue, and Ikhn-aton's scheme collapsed soon after his death about 1358 B.C.; the great 18th Dynasty then soon came to an end.

Another factor was beginning to change the balance of power. The Hittites in Asia Minor had discovered or learned the use of iron, and this acquisition led them to revolt against the domination of the Egyptians, who, in a reflective rather than expansive mood, tried to meet them by diplomatic agreements. The Hittites apparently maintained for some time a monopoly of the iron supplies, but traded this valuable metal among their neighbours.

With the passing-away of the supremacy of old materials, old methods, and old routes, and the rise of jealous daughter-groups at Tiryns and Mycenae, and probably with the mental fatigue induced by generations of effort and the accumulation of wealth, a dramatic change occurred in the position of Crete. Knossos fell about 1400 B.C. and, at that date according to Myres, or somewhat earlier according to Wace, there arose the Sixth City at Hissarlik, which was to be the Troy of Homer. Movements of people into Greece, chiefly from the north, occurred in the

fourteenth century B.C., and at this time begins the continuous
tradition of the heroes.

The discovery of processes to deal with iron was but one of
many-sided developments. The daughter-cities of Cretan culture on the Greek mainland were making many new things,
while cavalrymen, probably in central Europe, lengthened the
dagger into the slashing sword.

The rise of the mounted spearmen and swordsmen in central
Europe led to the supersession of the hammer or battle-axe,
which had been the typical weapon of the steppe-landers who
had dominated a mining area in Slovakia for a considerable time.
The new weapons used by horsemen seem to have opened up
larger possibilities of conquest and organization, and the
Hungarian basin of the Danube became a veritable melting-pot
of cultures, though still, characteristically, without that development of cities, which had for so long been a feature of the
civilization in the Near East and in the Indus basin. It is for
the present a useful hypothesis that, whereas the dagger and the
safety-pin are characteristic of the late Cretan and Mycenean
urban civilization, whence their use rapidly extended to the
Danubian lands, the sword of the cavalryman was, on the other
hand, a development in lands more devoted to the horse, though
it rapidly spread far and wide.

Meanwhile it is probable that the use of bronze was spreading
into Baltic lands and the British Isles, both of which would feel
the encouragement of fine warm seasons; it is an old English
proverb that 'drouth bringeth not dearth' and it is wet seasons
that our part of the world has to fear. In the course of time the
activities on the trading routes, that had long been developing
across central and west-central Europe, reached a high pitch, and
discoveries in the Alps indicate that the climate was warm. This
conclusion is also reached from a study of the pile-villages of the
Swiss lakes, which then attained their second phase of great

prosperity, with a highly developed bronze metallurgy. At much the same time the Baltic lands entered upon their period of wealth, probably in the twelfth century B.C., with gold and bronze work of high quality, and the development of a special type of sword. Apparently the attention of this civilization was turned more towards the tin supplies of Bohemia and the life of west-central Europe than towards the sea, for its characteristic objects do not occur in Britain, where the palstave became common and intercourse with Ireland was important. It is probable that a dry phase of climate and the exhaustion of the tin sands in Spain had for a time reduced the earlier importance of maritime movements along the Atlantic shores.

The open state of the Alpine passes, as the wealth of the Swiss pile-dwellings of the time indicate, encouraged frequent intercourse with Italy, which, in the thirteenth century B.C., was apparently attracting the attention of Mycenean traders; the spread of the safety-pin through Italy is an interesting feature, and reference has been made in Chapter 8 to the one-piece and the two-piece varieties and their divergent histories.

Meanwhile the Near East was obviously in a ferment. The power of the Hittites, with their iron supplies, drew attacks upon them, and about 1200 B.C. their empire collapsed. The Phrygian city of Hissarlik VI, or Troy, fell before the attacks of the Achaeans; we accept the traditional date of 1194 to 1184 B.C. for the Trojan War, though we note that Burn places it about 1100 B.C. In the thirteenth century B.C. the old organization of Egypt spent itself under Ramses II in colossal building enterprises; this marks the great influence of the old religion and its priesthood, which by the middle of the succeeding century became the supreme power in the land. This involved the decline of Egypt in an age when new weapons and new methods were spreading over the world. In his treaty with Hattushil about 1272 B.C. Ramses indicates his desire for iron. The disappearance of the old sea-power left the eastern Mediterranean in disorder, and 'peoples of the sea' attacked Egypt between 1230 and 1220 B.c., while at about the same time a Minoan civilization in Cyprus came to an end. About 1194 B.c. there was again an attack on Egypt. In Mesopotamia the rougher Assyrians acquired power over Babylon and began their great but chequered career as conquerors.

The latter part of the thirteenth or the beginning of the twelfth century B.c. was formerly often credited with the advance of the Israelites into Canaan under Joshua, but we have long thought this much too late a date, and in *Merchant Venturers in Bronze* we have reached, by argument, a conclusion very closely approximating to that which Garstang has developed through recent researches at Jericho, setting this event back well into the fourteenth century B.c. That the weakness of Egypt, Babylon, and the Hittites in the twelfth century B.c. may well have facilitated the settlement of Israelites in the Palestinian uplands is none the less probable. The movement of 'peoples of the sea' included the coming from the south-west of Asia Minor to south-west Palestine of the people known traditionally as the Philistines, while the Phoenician power was establishing itself on the coast farther north.

In the twelfth century B.c. the advancing movement of central-European peoples in several directions was actively continued, but apparently not in any strength towards the west Baltic, which was doubtless in the fullness of its power. The Lausitz people of the loess areas of south-east Germany, with the aid of the sword, drove their way through to Macedonia and Troy. Boeotians and Dorians advanced towards Greece. The Urn-fields people, with a culture based largely on that of Lausitz, occupied much of south Germany, and thus central Europe acquired a considerable increase of settled agricultural populations. Meanwhile the Achaeo-Mycenean culture of Greece, the old power of Babylon and Egypt, and the Hittite empire were dying or dead; on the other hand China was making great advances with the advent of the Chou Dynasty. In the eleventh century B.C. the Doric and Ionic migrations changed the face of the Aegean, the Philistines with iron swords temporarily dominated Palestine, before the kingdom of David and Solomon arose, and the Phoenicians came into greater prominence. In north-west Europe the great civilization of the Bronze Age in the Baltic was nearing the beginning of its decline, while apparently the British Isles were still little touched by the later cultural movements of the time.

One of the important developments of the Lausitz culture was that which adapted the idea of the socket to bronze axes, and the socketed axe and the sword can be followed separately into the British region; these are events that at the earliest estimates do not much antedate 1000 B.C., and some account has been included in this volume only because it is felt that the strict chronological scheme should not be too closely followed in dealing with obviously backward lands.

The end of the story in the Baltic lands and in Switzerland is a sad one of decline and fall connected with a change of climate giving cool wet summers, and no doubt long bad winters as well. The pile-dwellings near the Swiss lakes became submerged, the growth of ice seems to have closed some of the Alpine routes, the beech replaced the oak in several west-Baltic woodlands, and on high ground peat bogs spread at the expense of older forest. This change is no doubt the background for some of the legends of the Fimbul-Winter and the Twilight of the Gods, when the spear of Odin, that had already relegated the hammer of Thor to a secondary place, gave way in its turn before the decree of fate.

# INDEX

Abas, 27.
Abdi-khiba, 24.
Abydos, 25, 28.
Achaeans, 2, 3, 30–54, 59, 62, 63, 73, 78, 96, 138, 139, 146.
Achaia Phthiotis, 18, 26.
Achelous, R., 7.
Achilles, 33.
Acrisius, 27, 32.
Actaeon, 38.
Adad, &c., 21, 75.
Adlerberg, 103.
Adrastus, 39.
Adriatic Sea, 18, 80, 96–103.
Aeacus, 33.
Aegina, 33, 41.
Aegisthus, 63.
Aegyptus, 11, 12.
Aeneas, 46, 62, 68.
Aeolians, Aeolic, 3–6, 8, 18, 26–31, 38, 39, 78.
Aeolus, 27, 33.
Aerope, 37.
Aetolia, 33.
Agamemnon, 2, 33, 37–44, 58–63.
Agave, 37.
Agni, 139.
Agrigentum, 9.
Ahhiyava, 2, 26, 42.
Ajax, 33.
Akarsalla, 61.
Alabastronpolis, 24.
Alasya, 36, 56.
Alb, R., 104.
Alcaeus, 37.
Alcmene, 37.
Aleppo, 25, 29.
Alsace, 104.
Alshi or Alzi, 20, 23, 64, 66.
Alybe, 44, 55.
Amazons, 32, 59.
amber, 80, 106, 118, 126.
Amenopet, 21, 79.
Amenhotep, 11, 21, 22, 29, 63, 65.
Amen-mose, 21, 34.
Ammon, 24, 34, 60–6, 74, 75, 79.
Amor, 59.
Amorites, 25, 56.
Amphilochus, 39.
Amphitryon, 37.
Andreus, 26.
Andromeda, 32.
Antaravas, 26.
Antioch, 60.
Aramaeans, 3, 79.
Arcadia, Arcadian, 3, 4, 5, 12, 18, 36, 63.
Arcesius, 33.
Ares, 33, 37.
Argeus, Mt., 64.
Argives, 2.
Argo, 48.
Argolis, 2, 5, 11–16, 17, 27, 32–9, 46, 58.
Argonauts, 48.

Argos, 32, 39, 74.
Argus, 91.
Ariadne, 13.
Aristaeus, 38.
Arne, 73.
Arnuandash, 21–3, 25, 36.
Artatama, 22, 23.
Arvad, 29, 56.
Aryans, 23, 40, 94, 97, 135–40.
Arzawa, 20.
Ashur, &c., 21, 22, 61, 64, 75, 79, 80.
Askalon, 34.
As-su-va, 18, 36.
Assyrian, 11, 20–3, 57–67, 75, 79, 147.
Asterius, 27, 31.
Asy, 18.
Athamas, 26, 38.
Athens, 14, 15, 49, 74, 76, 78, 96.
Aton, 24.
Atreus, 2, 35–7, 39, 41, 42.
Attarissyas, 2, 42.
Attica, 3, 7, 32, 74.
Aulis, 12, 13, 40.
Aunjetitz, 82–92, 103, 104, 115.
Autonöe, 37, 38.
Auvernier, 109, 110.
Axius, R., 44.
Ayavalas, 26.
Aye, 24.

Babylon, 3, 11, 21–3, 61–4, 66, 67, 147, 148.
Baia de arama, 85.
Balkans, 5, 50, 85, 97, 103.
Baltic Sea, 80, 85, 93, 100, 106–15, 118–22, 132, 133, 145, 147, 148.
barley, 137, 138.
Batum, 55.
Bavaria, 103, 134.
Beaker people, 85, 122.
Beäs, 140.
Bellerophon, 32, 36.
Berne, 108.
Beyrout, 28.
Bharates, 140.
Bias, 39.
Biggaia, 36.
Black Earth Lands, 8, 49.
Blinkenberg, C., 89.
Boeotia, 3–7, 11, 16, 42, 44, 73, 147.
Boghaz Keui, 2, 26, 30, 55.
Bohemia, 80, 85, 103–18, 122, 146.
Bohúslan, 122.
Bonn, 130.
Bosnia, 50, 103.
Boubasta, 6, 7.
Brandenburg, 109.
Bremelau, 107.
Brenner pass, 80.
Brittany, 113, 122–9, 132.

Brooks, C. E. P., 133.
Bryges, 32.
Buboshta, 70, 72.
Buddha, 95.
Burn, A. R., 1, 2, 9, 13, 15, 58, 68, 146.
Burna-Buriash, 21, 23.
Bury, J. B., 42, 46.
Byblos, 65, 66.

Cadmeians, Cadmus, 11, 14, 16, 18, 27, 31, 33, 37, 39, 70, 73.
Calabria, 9, 10.
Calydnae, 42.
Campylus, R., 7.
Canaan, 24, 147.
Cappadocia, 20, 58, 64.
Carchemish, 20, 25, 29, 56, 59.
Caria, 2, 17, 31, 42, 44, 57, 58.
Carmalas, 20.
Carmel, Mt., 60.
Carpathus, 42.
Castor of Rhodes, 68.
Casus, 42.
Cecrops, 15.
Chaeronea, 74.
Chalcas, 39.
Chaldaeans, 79.
Chalybes, 55.
Charybdis, 90.
Chauchitza, 70, 72.
Childe, V. G., 58, 86, 88, 92.
Chou Dynasty, 3, 141, 148.
Chrysippus, 35.
Cilicians, 29, 39, 60.
Cithaeron, Mt., 37.
Clay, R. C. C., 123.
Cleola, 37.
Clytemnestra, 13, 63.
Cnidos, 57.
Codrus, 74.
Colchis, 48.
Commagene, 66.
Confucius, 95, 141.
Copais, L., 5.
copper, 1, 82, 85, 86, 97, 113, 114, 118, 121, 126.
Corinth, 3, 5, 6, 7, 11, 18, 27, 32, 41, 46, 68, 73, 74, 78.
Cos, 42.
Crawford, O. G. S., 124.
Crete, 1–19, 27, 30–41, 58, 76, 78, 95, 143–5.
Cretheus, 27.
Crissa, 74.
Curle, A., 114.
Çutudri, 140.
Cycladic, culture, 5, 47.
Cyme, 78.
Cyprus, 4, 27, 36, 63, 69, 147.
Cyrus, 95.

Daedalus, 9.
Dana, 58, 60.
Danaans, 2, 12, 13, 27, 33, 58.
Danaus, 11–13, 27.

Danube, R., 48, 84, 85, 88–97, 100, 102, 103, 107, 145.
Daphnus, R., 74.
Dardanians, 18, 19.
Darius, 95.
Darmstadt, 104.
David, 60, 79, 148.
Delta, 27, 33–5, 60, 61, 66, 67, 74.
Der, 60.
Deverel-Rimbury, 123, 125, 130.
Diodorus Sic., 9, 10, 27, 30, 68.
Diomedes, 33.
Dipylon gate, 76.
Djakarat, 58.
Dnimini, 8, 18, 70, 71, 95.
Dodona, 73.
Dor, 66.
Dorians, Doric, Doris, 3–5, 12, 18, 27–31, 41, 68, 70–8, 147.
Dorus, 27.
Dudkhalia, 2, 21, 34, 35, 36.
Dyaus, 139.

Eberswalde, 120.
Echion, 37.
Edom, 64.
Ekereth, 29.
Ekhelm, G., 90.
Ekwesh, 34.
Elamites, 61.
Elbe, R., 80, 82.
Electryon, 37.
Eli, 64.
Elis, 12, 18, 33, 35, 42.
El-Kab, 63.
Enlil, &c., 21, 22, 23, 62, 63, 75.
Ephyra, 27, 32.
Eratosthenes, 1, 2.
Eriba-Adad, 21, 75.
Erösd, 51.
Erwenet, 29.
Eshnunna, 137.
Eteocles, 26, 39.
Etruscans, 34, 68, 96.
Euboea, 3, 7, 12, 41.
Euphrates, 20, 22, 59, 64, 95.
Europa, Europus, 14, 15, 30, 31.
Eurysthenes, 37.
Eusebius, 68, 69.
Euxine Sea, 46–8, 55, 99.
Evans, Sir Arthur, 9, 10.
Evans, Estyn, 124, 125, 129.

fibulae, 17, 85, 89–93, 98–100, 114–21, 122.
Fimbul-Winter, 148.
Firdausi, 135.
Forrer, E., 2.
Fox, Cyril, 132.
Franconia, 80.
Frankfort, H., 137.
Frankfurt, 107.
Fribourg, 108.

Galilee, 24.
Gallipoli, 47.
Gams, H., 134.

Garstang, J., 147.
Gebel Zebara, 25.
Gemeinlebarn, 90, 92.
Gerar, 53, 54.
Glotz, G., 9.
gold, 25, 28, 48, 85, 110, 115, 117–20, 122, 146.
Gold Country, 34.
Golden Fleece, 48.
Gowland, W., 54.
Greeks, 3, 4, 8, 23, 39, 40, 55, 64, 69, 79, 80.

Hagenau, 104.
Haliacmon, R., 6, 7.
Hall, H. R., 57, 58.
Hallstatt, 108, 109, 121.
Halys, R., 2, 44, 55.
Haran, 20.
Harappa, 137.
Harmais, 13.
Harmhab, 13, 16, 21, 24.
Harmonia, 37.
Harris papyrus, 60, 63.
Hatshepsut, 144.
Hattushil, 11, 20, 21, 29, 30, 34, 35, 53, 147.
Hauran, 24.
Heathery Burn Cave, 126.
Hebrews, 3, 64, 79, 96, 134.
Helen, 44, 63.
Hellas, 70.
Hellenes, 3, 7, 11, 16–19, 70, 78.
Hellespont, 18, 32, 46, 47, 49, 59.
Henttoui, 74.
Hephaistos, 41.
Heracles, 37, 73.
Hermes, 41.
Hermione, 63.
Herodotus, 9, 10, 14, 27, 68, 70, 75.
Hesiod, 62.
Hesse, 104.
Heurtley, W. A., 6.
Hippodamia, 33.
Hissarlik, 1, 5, 6, 18, 19, 32, 36, 40, 49, 51, 68, 72, 85, 95, 144, 146.
Histiaeotis, 27.
Hittites, 2, 3, 8, 11, 19–25, 28–31, 34–6, 39–42, 53–5, 58–60, 64, 66, 79, 144–8.
Homer, 40, 41, 49, 55, 73, 144.
Hor-Psibkhenno, 21, 79.
horses, 51, 80, 86, 93, 107, 113, 118, 119, 138, 143, 144.
Hrihor, 21, 66, 74.
Hrozny, F., 2.
Hyria, 9.

Ida, Mt., 19, 29.
Idomeneus, 14, 15.
Ikhn-aton, 13, 21, 22, 24, 96, 144.
Ilbaba-shum-iddin, 21, 61, 62.
Iliad, 42, 44, 47, 51.
Ilion, 32.
Illyria, 18, 97.
Indo-European, 3–8, 18, 135.

Ino, 37.
Ionian, 3–6, 8, 16–18, 32, 41, 44, 57, 78, 148.
Iphicles, 37.
Iphigenia, 13.
Iranians, 96, 135, 138.
iron, 30, 53–5, 109, 121, 144–8.
Iron Age, 90, 97, 101, 103, 109, 111, 128, 131.
Iron Gates, 85.
Irriya, 61.
Isin, 63, 75, 79.
Israel, 8, 25, 34, 40, 69, 80, 95, 147.
Issus, 58.
Ithaca, 33.
Itti-marduk-zer-mati, 21.

Jahveh, 96.
Jerusalem, 24.
Jericho, 147.
Jocasta, 38.
Jordan, 25.
Joshua, 25, 147.
Judaea, 60.
Jura, 80, 108, 109.

Kadashman, &c., 21, 22.
Kadesh, 24, 28, 29.
Kaiomurs, 135.
Kaldu, 79.
Kamikos, 9.
Kara-Indash, 11, 21, 22.
Karduniash, 61.
Karnak, 24, 25, 29, 30, 74.
Kassites, 3, 11, 22, 23, 61–3.
Kehek, 56.
Khale-wa, 55.
Kharrians, 11, 20, 23.
Khatti, 56.
Khattussas, 2, 31, 55.
Kili-Teshub, 66.
Kissuwadna, 11, 20, 25, 29, 30, 54.
Knossos, 1, 9–17, 27, 31, 32, 37, 38, 69, 78, 95, 99, 144.
Knum, 61.
Kode, 29, 56.
Koiranos, 36, 42.
Korakou, 6, 73, 74.
Kossinna, G., 111.
Kronos, 41.
Kummukh, 66.
Kurigalzu, 21, 23.
Kurvanas, 36.

La-as-pa, 26, 36.
Labdacus, 38.
Laconia, 27.
Laius, 38.
Laodamus, 33.
Laomedon, 32, 36.
Lao-Tse, 95.
Lappenabsatzbeil, 125.
Lausitz culture, 48, 68, 72, 73, 76, 82–93, 122, 128, 147.
Leaf, W., 42, 46, 47.
Learchis, 38.
Lebanon, 24, 66.
Leleges, 58.
Lesbos, 12, 26, 27, 36, 78.

Levant, 60.
Libyans, 33-5, 56, 60, 61, 99.
Ligures, 100.
Locris, 4, 7, 12, 18, 26, 41.
Lovasberény, 83.
Lycians, 29, 32-4, 36, 44, 57.
Lydia, 44, 68, 69.
Lykki, 34.
Lysimache, 39.

Macedonia, 5-7, 32, 70-6, 93, 147.
Maeonians, 29, 44, 69.
Main, R., 107.
Mainz, 104, 107.
Makare-Mutemhat, 75.
Maliac Gulf, 6, 7, 17, 18, 70.
Malis, 4, 7.
Manetho, 13.
Marduk, &c., 21, 61, 66, 75.
Marmora, Sea of, 32.
Marshall, Sir John, 136-8.
Masaherti, 75.
Maspere, G., 58.
Mattiuazza, 20, 23.
Mazaka, 64.
Mazki, 64.
Mediterranean, 67, 88, 93, 97-9, 132, 134.
Megapenthes, 39.
Megara, 74.
Megaron, 49-51, 82, 95.
Megiddo, 24.
Melampus, 39.
Melicertes, 38.
Meli-Shipak, 21, 61.
Menelaus, 33, 37, 44, 62, 63.
Menestheus, 14.
Menkheperre, 21, 75, 78, 79.
Merneptah, 3, 21, 34, 35.
Mery-ey, 34.
Mesara, 10.
Mesech, 64.
Mesheneth, 29.
Meshwesh, 60.
Mesopotamia, 22, 79, 95, 137, 138, 143, 147.
Minos, Minoa, 9, 10, 14, 15, 30-2, 37.
Minotaur, 13-15.
Minyan ware, 5, 16, 17, 72.
Mitanni, 11, 20, 22.
Mitra, 139.
Mohenjo-daro, 136, 137, 142.
Montelius, O., 112, 114, 118, 119.
Montenegro, 51.
Mopsus, 39.
Morava, R., 18.
Mörigen, 109, 110.
Moschi, 32, 64.
Müller, S., 85, 112, 114-19, 121.
Munthe, H., 133.
Murshil ii, 21-3, 25, 26, 58.
Muski, 32, 64, 66.
Mutallu, 21, 26, 29.
Mu Wang, 142.
Mycenae, 9, 11, 12, 16, 17, 32-9, 42, 46-9, 52, 73, 74, 95, 99, 144, 145.

Myres, J. L., 1-6, 12, 13, 15, 19, 27, 33, 41, 48-50, 57, 58, 82, 89, 100, 134, 144.
Mysians, 29, 44.

Nabu-shum-libur, 21, 79.
Naharin, 29.
Naupactus, 74.
Nausithous, 33.
Naxos, 12, 13.
Nebuchadnezzar, 21.
Nebuchadrezzar I, 64, 67.
Nestor, 42.
Nesubenebded, 66, 67, 74, 79.
Ninurta, &c., 21, 61, 75.
Nisyrus, 42.
Nordhagen, R., 134.
Nubia, 29, 34.
Nuges, 29.
Nürnberg, 107.

Oassos, 58.
Oaxos, 58.
Oberbayern, 104.
Oberpfalz, 104.
Oder, R., 82.
Odin, 93, 148.
Odysseus, 33, 44, 49, 62.
Oedipus, 39.
Oeneus, 33.
Oenomaus, 33.
Olympia, 6.
Olympus, Mt., 12, 18, 27, 30, 70.
Orchomenos, 5-7, 26, 38, 95.
Orestes, 63, 64.
Orontes, R., 26, 27, 29, 59.
Orsi, P., 97.
Ossa, Mt., 12, 18, 27, 30, 70.

Paeonians, 18.
Painozem, 21, 75, 78, 79.
Palestine, 24-32, 53, 57-64, 79, 134, 147, 148.
palstaves, 124, 125, 127, 146.
Pamphylia, 4, 42.
Pannonia, 84.
Paphlagonia, 55.
Paris, 44.
Parnassus, 68.
Pashe, 63.
Paul, St., 96.
Pedasus, 29.
Peet, T. E., 98.
Pelasgians, 27, 57, 58, 69.
Pelcset, 57.
Peleus, 42.
Peloponnese, 4, 5, 12, 16-18, 32, 36, 41, 48, 50, 57, 63, 64, 68, 72-5, 78.
Pelops, 33, 35, 41, 57.
Peneus, R., 5, 7, 30.
Pentewere, 61.
Pentheus, 37, 38.
Perieres, 27.
Perire, 31.
Perseus, 2, 32, 35, 37, 39.
Persian Gulf, 79.
Pettersson, O., 133.
Phaeacia, 33.
Pharaoh, 15.

Philistines, 3, 8, 23, 40, 55, 57, 60, 69, 79, 80, 148.
Philochorus, 13, 14.
Phocis, 4, 7.
Phoenicians, 3, 69, 78, 147, 148.
Phrygians, 32, 33, 36, 40, 44, 48, 49, 53, 59, 64, 69, 146.
Phthia, 18, 42.
Phthiotis, 4, 7, 12.
Phylakopi, 95.
Piankh, 74, 75.
Pidasa, 29.
Pile, 113.
Pindus, Mt., 7, 27, 68-72, 74, 76.
Pisa, 33.
Pisidia, 58.
Pleisthenes, 37.
Pleuron, 33.
P-l-s-t-, 56, 57, 59.
Pokesdown, 123.
Polydorus, 37, 38.
Polynices, 39.
Pomerania, 109.
Pontus, 55.
Poseidon, 33, 62.
Pottier, E., 8.
Priam, 32, 36, 44, 59, 62.
Prithivi, 139.
Proetus, 27, 32, 39.
Propontis, 47.
Psibkhenno, 21, 74, 75.
Pterelaus, 37.
Pteria, 2, 55.
Pterseus, 2.
Pulisati, 57.
Purukuzzi, 64, 66.
Pylos, 42.

Ramses I & II, 21, 24-7, 29, 30, 33, 34, 53, 54, 56, 59, 60, 61, 63-6, 146.
Red Sea, 60, 78.
Reinecke, P., 89, 90, 99, 100, 112.
Rhine, R., 81, 104, 107, 130, 132.
Rhodes, 42.
Rhodians, 69.
Rhön, R., 104.
Ridgeway, Sir W., 33.
Rimisharma, 25.
Rolf the Ganger, 52.
Rumania, 8, 85.
Russia, 8, 40, 47, 51, 81, 83, 97, 134.

Sagalassus, 34, 58.
Salamis, 41.
salt, 107, 108.
Sangarius, R., 59.
Sarasvati, R., 136.
Sardis, 34, 56.
Saul, 79.
Sauter, F., 104.
Sayce, A. H., 2, 58.
Scamander, R., 47.
Scandinavia, 106, 114, 115, 120, 133.
Schleswig-Holstein, 87, 106.

# 152      *Index*

Scythia, 134.
Seddin, 120.
Seelenloch, 83.
Semele, 37, 38.
Semitic speech, 25.
Seti, 21, 24–6, 28, 34, 35, 56.
Setnakht, 21, 35.
Shakalsha, 58.
Shalmaneser, 21, 80.
Shamshi-Adad, 21, 75, 79.
Shang dynasty, 3.
Shardana, 33, 56.
Shardina, 29.
Shaush-shatar, 23.
Shekelesh, Sh-k-l-sh, 34, 56, 58, 59.
Shekhlal, 58.
Sherden, 29, 34, 56.
Shetland, 114.
Shiloh, 64.
Shishak, 79.
Shubbiluliuma, 20, 21, 22, 25.
Shulmanu-asharid, 21, 80.
Shunash-shirra, 25.
Shutrul-Nakhunte, 62.
Shuttarna, 23.
Siamon, 21, 79.
Sicily, 9, 10, 14–16, 34, 97–99, 102.
Siculi, 98.
Sidon, 63, 78.
silver, 30, 44.
Simois, R., 19.
Sippar, 75.
Sisyphus, 27, 32.
Slovakia, 82, 84, 85, 93, 118, 145.
Smyrna, 78.
Solomon, 79, 148.
Solymi, 36.
Spain, 98, 122, 134, 146.
Sparta, 44, 78.
Spercheios, R., 6, 7, 17, 70–2, 76.
Sthenelos, 37.
Strabo, 67.
Susagi, 23.
swords, 85–93, 101, 105, 109–12, 115–19, 124, 129–32, 138, 145–7.
Syme, 42.
Syria, 16, 20, 22, 25, 26, 28, 29, 35, 56, 58–60, 63, 64, 79, 95, 99.

Talaus, 39.
Tanis, 66, 74, 79.
Taphos, 37.
Tarkhundarush, 20.
Ta-ro-i-sa, 36.
Tarsiyas, 2.
Taurus Mts., 11, 20.
Tavagalavas, 26.
Tectamus, 27.
Temes-Kubin, 83.
Teresh, 34.
Terremare, 100–3.
Teucrians, 19, 58.
Tewosret, 34.
Thalassocracies, 68.
Thebes, 11, 16, 18, 24, 28, 30, 37, 39, 63–5, 73, 74.
Thekel, 58.
Thermi, 95.
Thersites, 51.
Theseus, 13, 14, 16.
Thesprotia, 73, 74.
Thessalians, 73, 74.
Thessaly, 4–8, 12, 18, 27, 42, 68, 70, 72, 73.
Thor, 93, 149.
Thrace, Thracians, 40, 44, 69.
Thuringia, 103, 104, 109.
Thutmose III, 18, 28, 74, 144.
Thyestes, 35, 41.
Thymoitadae, 13.
Ticino, 108.
Tiglath-pileser, 21, 66, 67, 75, 79.
Tigris, R., 23.
tin, 1, 80, 85, 97, 122, 126, 138, 146.
Tiryns, 6, 12, 16, 27, 32, 39, 49, 73, 74, 95, 144.
Tisamenos, 64, 68.
Tiy, 24, 61.
Transcaucasia, 48.
Transjordania, 25.
Transylvania, 48, 49, 85.
Troad, 19, 44, 60.
Troezen, 12, 13, 15, 16.
Trojan War, 4, 14, 33, 44–6, 68, 146.
Troy, 1–3, 10–14, 19, 32, 36, 40–3, 44, 47, 49, 55, 58, 59, 62, 68, 69, 73, 95, 98, 144–7.
T-r-s-y-s, 2.
Tushratta, 20, 22.
Tut-enkh-amen, 1, 21, 53.
*tutulus*, 117.

Twilight of the Gods, 148.
Tyana, 58, 64.
Tymphrastus, Mt., 7.
Tyre, 63, 66, 78.
Tyrsenians, 34, 68.
Uashasha, Uasha-sha, 58.
Ur, 53.
Urn-fields, 83, 104, 107–9, 120, 122, 123, 131, 147.
Valais, 108.
Vardar, R., 5, 44.
Vardaroftsa, 70–2.
Vikings, 51.
Villafrati, 97.
Villanova culture, 99.
Vinča, 89.
Vipaç, 140.
Virgil, 40.
Vistula, R., 119.
Vogelsberg, 104.
Wace, A. J. B., 6, 19, 144.
Wadi Alaki, 25, 28.
Wainwright, G. A., 53.
Warlike Prince, The, 141.
Washasha, W-sh-sh, 56, 58, 59.
Woolley, C. L., 53.
Wörms, 103.
Wu-wang, 141.
Xanthus, R., 44.
Xenophon, 58.
Xerxes, 57.
Yenoam, 24.
Yeshil Irmak, 55.
Yin dynasty, 3.
Zaban, 61.
Zagros, Mts., 137.
Zakar-baal, 66.
Zakkal, 58.
Zakkaru, 58, 66.
Zakro, 58.
Zarathustra, 96.
Zedkhonsefankh, 75.
Zeus, 30, 31, 33, 41.
Zikhria, 58.
Zipparla, 2, 42.
Z-kk-r, 56, 58, 60.
Zoroaster, 96.
Zürich, 109, 110.

PRINTED IN GREAT BRITAIN AT THE UNIVERSITY PRESS, OXFORD
BY JOHN JOHNSON, PRINTER TO THE UNIVERSITY